'A wise, thoughtful and very readable series of essays from someone who spent his working life at the forefront of nature conservation, and has now shared his accumulated wisdom with the rest of us.'　　　－ Stephen Moss, author and naturalist

'A highly enjoyable read – informative, thought-provoking and above all balanced. Ian Carter wears his copious knowledge extremely lightly.'
－ Lev Parikian, author of *Into The Tangled Bank* and *Why Do Birds Suddenly Disappear?*

'A wonderful collection of heartfelt, insightful essays – each one like a privileged chat about the highs, lows and many conundrums of three decades working with nature, from one of its most personable and pragmatic champions. We need people like Ian.'
－ Dr Amy-Jane Beer, naturalist, writer and campaigner

'*Human, Nature* deserves to be read very widely . . . here is a book that considers all the most pressing questions we face as we attempt to understand and fundamentally change our relationship with the natural world. Most importantly, it makes the connections between them, and quietly asserts the need for us to start making more connections – between sites, whole landscapes, and each other.'
－ Matt Merritt, editor of *Bird Watching* magazine and author of *A Sky Full of Birds*

'I love the warmth and refreshing candour of Ian's writing. Readable and relatable – this is an enriching book, from a reliable witness. Highly recommended.'

– Conor Jameson, author and conservationist

'Ian Carter offers highly readable musings on the most pressing issues facing Britain's beleaguered wildlife. Balancing obvious expertise with refreshing honesty . . . His infectious passion for the great outdoors sings from every page.'

– Dan Eatherley, author of *Invasive Aliens*

'A deeply engaging account of our complex relationship with the natural world. Drawing on his conservation expertise and lifelong passion for wildlife, Ian explores a wide range of contentious issues and shares the joy of reconnecting with nature in this enlightening, honest and very accessible book.'

– Nic Wilson, nature writer and *Guardian* Country Diarist

'It has been a real pleasure for me as a country-dweller to read Ian Carter's work, because he somehow tells it like it is more than any other rural writer I know . . . What he describes is not a fancied landscape cloaked with nostalgia or the ethereal pastures of the far-fetched poet, but a very real place in which birds fly and die in equal measure.'   – Martin Hesp, journalist and novelist

'One of the best accounts I have ever read of the complex relationship between humans and wildlife, celebrating the huge benefits it can bring and full of wise comment on the dilemmas it often poses.'   – Jonathan Elphick, natural history author and editor

Human, Nature

Ian Carter recently left Natural England after a career as an ornithologist spanning twenty-five years. He was closely involved with the Red Kite reintroduction programme in England and has a particular interest in the conservation of birds of prey, bird reintroductions and wildlife management more generally. He is especially interested in the cultural aspects of nature conservation and how these interact with science to influence our attitudes towards the natural world. He has written articles for various wildlife magazines including *British Birds* and *British Wildlife*, and has co-authored many papers in scientific journals. He also wrote *The Red Kite* (Arlequin Press, second edition 2007) and, with Dan Powell, *The Red Kite's Year* (Pelagic Publishing 2019). He has been on the Editorial Board of *British Birds* for more than twenty years. Although not a habitual note taker in the field, he keeps a wildlife journal and has written something in it (however dull) every day for over thirty-five years.

Human, Nature

A Naturalist's Thoughts on Wildlife and Wild Places

IAN CARTER

PELAGIC PUBLISHING

Published by Pelagic Publishing
PO Box 874
Exeter
EX3 9BR
UK

www.pelagicpublishing.com

Human, Nature: A Naturalist's Thoughts on Wildlife and Wild Places

ISBN 978-1-78427-257-9 (Hbk)
ISBN 978-1-78427-258-6 (ePub)
ISBN 978-1-78427-259-3 (ePDF)
ISBN 978-1-78427-260-9 (Audio)

A CIP record for this book is available from the British Library

Cover image © Angela Harding
Section opener images © Richard Allen

Typeset in Adobe Caslon Pro by Palimpsest Book Production Ltd,
Falkirk, Stirlingshire

To those sharing the wildlife encounters (welcome or otherwise) on our annual family holiday: Ali and Ben; Jacks, Jon, Danny and Katie; Margaret and Brian; and Hazel.

CONTENTS

CONFLICTS

WILD PLACES

ACKNOWLEDGEMENTS

My first proper job in conservation started thirty years ago with the old Nature Conservancy Council's Seabirds at Sea team. Mark Tasker and Andy Webb were my mentors and, in their very different ways, provided a fantastic introduction to working in nature conservation. A few years later I joined English Nature (now Natural England) and spent two years working closely with Callum Rankine on Special Protection Areas and Ramsar sites. After that, I moved on to the Red Kite reintroduction, a programme that has involved dozens of people over the years. It would be invidious to single out individuals, but all involved can take great pride in what has been achieved.

I am grateful to a large number of my former colleagues at Natural England and in other conservation organisations for lively discussions, over the years, on many of the subjects covered in this book, including Andy Brown, Alistair Crowle, Allan Drewitt, Phil Grice, Matt Heydon, Stephen Murphy, Richard Saunders and Nigel Shelton.

Alistair Crowle read the whole text, challenging ideas that were not fully thought through and making insightful and helpful comments throughout. My wife, Hazel, read various early drafts, and her efforts have spared readers from some of the more esoteric and unsupportable ideas. She also identified sections with confused thinking and persuaded me to either improve or remove them.

I am very grateful to Hugh Brazier for reading through an early draft and providing thoughtful and insightful feedback. He helped convince me that the themes I was writing about were worth pursuing as this book. Later in the process he did his usual thorough job of editing the text, hunting down mangled sentences and making many helpful suggestions to improve the flow of the writing. Nigel Massen, David Hawkins and Moira Reid at Pelagic Publishing were also a pleasure to work with, ensuring that the journey to publication was as smooth as possible.

Mark Avery published versions of several of these essays on his influential blog *Standing up for Nature*. Three more were developed from pieces published under the *BB eye* feature which starts every issue of the journal *British Birds*.

I am especially grateful to my parents Brian and Margaret. They encouraged an early interest in wild things and allowed me to roam free in the local woods and fields in a way that would be unthinkable for kids today. They have also been willing participants in discussions about wildlife and conservation over five decades (and counting).

It has been invaluable, over the years, to have two fresh young minds to bounce ideas off, and I'm eternally grateful to my two children Ali and Ben for their sustained interest in the natural world. The topic of wildlife and its conservation enlivened many a car journey, though we never did resolve the question that came up most often: are there more tree leaves or blades of grass on the planet? Perhaps someone out there knows.

INTRODUCTION

As well as having a lifelong interest in the natural world, I've always been fascinated by the varied and complex ways in which people interact with wildlife. It's difficult to imagine another area of interest where human viewpoints vary so much from person to person. For some people, wildlife is to be enjoyed, cherished and protected at all costs. For others it is most noticeable when it causes problems or gets in the way. And for others still it is highly valued as a resource: it is there to be exploited, sometimes in a sustainable way, sometimes not. When walking in the countryside we may encounter people with binoculars taking great delight in watching the local wildlife, and we may come across someone with shotgun in hand who values wildlife primarily for the sport it provides. On several major wetlands close to our old house in the Cambridgeshire Fens, these two groups were sometimes out in force at the same time during the winter shooting season, offering the starkest of contrasts.

As part of my role as an ornithologist with Natural England I had to deal with all manner of enquiries about birds. These provided a daily reminder of the huge differences that exist in our attitudes towards wildlife. One call might be from someone complaining about birds (large gulls, perhaps) and wanting to know if we could help to kill or remove them. The next might be from an individual who valued those same birds highly and was concerned that they were not sufficiently protected. I'd be asked by one person how best to kill Magpies because they were unwelcome destroyers of breeding songbirds. And then another would ask me how to stop the next-door neighbour from killing Magpies. When it comes to birds of prey, views are often highly polarised. The Red Kite has been helped to make a remarkably rapid comeback to the skies of Britain, while during the same period the Hen Harrier has been helped to the edge of extinction as a breeding bird in England. The contrast could hardly be any greater.

Trying to balance opposing viewpoints is tricky, but of far greater concern is the increasing number of people for whom wildlife has little significance. We've all seen survey results in the media showing that most children no longer know the names for a wide range of common and 'familiar' species. Many kids leave primary school having never consciously set eyes on a newt or a Blue Tit or a Primrose. They have no idea what these species look like and they probably don't much care. Even prospective zoology students struggle to recognise common animals. They are encouraged to attend a basic natural history field course in their first year at university to help them get up to speed.

Like many people of my generation, I developed a love of nature through being allowed to explore it from an early age. I was lucky on two counts. I was brought up in places where there was wildlife all around, within easy walking distance of our home. And I benefited from the fact that, in those days, kids were generally free to roam around outdoors doing their own thing. It's a bit of a stretch to say that it was 'cool' to be interested in wildlife. But it was certainly normal to spend time, either alone or with others, with nothing more by way of entertainment than what the local countryside had to offer. Almost every small child has an intrinsic fascination with wild creatures. There can't be many of us who didn't spend time as kids dipping nets into ponds and turning over stones, trying to find interesting animals to entertain us and alarm our parents. Increasingly, this in-built curiosity is stifled at an early age by competition from other forms of entertainment, and because exploring the local country-side is frowned upon – by parents concerned about safety, and by peers who are unimpressed by expressions of affection for the natural world.

A recurring theme in this book is the fact that wildlife and the experience of 'wildness' are getting more and more difficult to come by in Britain, particularly in the lowlands, where farming is ever more intensive and human impacts dominate. Part of the problem is that landscapes degrade so slowly that we don't really notice. We subconsciously adjust our expectations to what we have left, rather than mourning what has been lost. It's now more than a hundred years since the last surviving Passenger Pigeon died in Cincinnati Zoo. This was once the world's most abundant bird, with flocks of millions darkening the skies of North America. On this side of the Atlantic we've been without the spectacular Great Auk for a few decades longer. Try to imagine being able to visit the densely packed breeding colonies of this huge, flight-less species – the 'penguin' of the northern hemisphere. I certainly find it tricky to picture the scene and, for that reason, it's diffi-cult to care very much about it. We make the most of what we have, partly because we have no choice and partly because our brains are so well adapted to deal with situations as they are, rather than as they might have been. If future generations of British birdwatchers have to make do without Turtle Doves, Cuckoos and Nightingales, they will adjust their expectations in the same way. Only from our perspective, now, being able to see these birds for ourselves, can we appreciate what they would be missing.

In Britain, the loss of wildlife in recent decades has led to an increasing contrast between the ever more impoverished 'wider countryside' and our carefully managed nature reserves, which can teem with wildlife. Despite that contrast, I find I get more pleasure from watching wildlife away from reserves. I think it's because watching wildlife is, for me, about escaping from everyday life and the all-pervading influence of humans in a world that we dominate. That sense of escape is difficult to find in our modern flagship nature reserves, with their hides, boardwalks, information boards and abundant visitors.

Not everyone who appreciates wildlife feels that way, of course, and we all approach the subject in our own way. Some are drawn to focus on just one species, with an urge to find out as much as they possibly can about it. Others spend their time dashing around the countryside trying to see as many different species as possible, pausing to watch an animal for little longer than is required to confirm its identity. For others still, an interest in wildlife is there but is more casual. Wildlife in the garden and in the local countryside (or the local town) provides a backdrop to other activities but is appreciated nonetheless and would be greatly missed if it wasn't there.

One of the things that makes an interest in the natural world so rewarding, and I would argue sets it apart from all other interests, is the fact that wildlife is all around us. It is with us constantly. It can grab our attention, unexpectedly, at any time. We see wildlife in some form every day, whether that involves going somewhere specifically to watch it, or snatching moments as and when the opportunities arise. It might be from the car, or from the train, or when peering out of a dreary office window. While writing this today, I've been reaffirming the point I'm trying to make. I've been repeatedly distracted by birds on the feeders outside my window. And by the now familiar autumn build-up of introduced Harlequin Ladybirds inside the house. They are all heading for the corners of the window frames, where they will spend the winter huddled in tight clusters, just above my desk. The trappings of a serious interest in wildlife might give the impression of a hobby: the binoculars, field guides, magazines and the like. But, in reality, it's more a way of life. It makes life richer and more fulfilling and, as increasingly demonstrated by the latest research, it even prolongs life through the enhanced sense of wellbeing that it fosters.

I've always enjoyed writing about wildlife, and this book is, in part, a natural extension of the wildlife journals I've kept assiduously for over three decades. During that time, I've written something about wildlife every day, even if it's nothing more exciting than an autumn Goldcrest in the garden, a decent count of Brown Hares, or a Marsh Harrier patrolling the drain that runs by the house. While these notes were helpful in jogging my memory, the fact that they are handwritten meant countless wasted hours trying to track down a particular event. Initially, I cursed the fact that I hadn't adopted a more systematic approach and used a computer so that I could search for particular species or places. But, on reflection, I realise that I don't keep this written record for its reference value. I keep it because there is something remarkably therapeutic and life-affirming about watching wildlife and noting down the interesting or the unusual. I'm convinced I get a better sense of what I saw (and the feelings evoked) through these handwritten accounts than would be the case with a more formal, word-processed document. If that doesn't sound logical then it fits very well with the broader aspects of our relationships with the natural world. These are based on complex and unpredictable interactions involving childhood experience, cultural associations and the effects of thousands of years of evolution on the human mind.

This book is divided into four parts made up of short, essay-style chapters, each of which can be read in isolation. Nevertheless, I hope that the individual chapters build gradually into a more coherent whole. The aim is to provide an overview of the various ways in which I interact with wildlife and how that leads me to think about my relationship with the natural world. Most of the early chapters were written over a period of several years when we lived in the flatlands of the Cambridgeshire Fens. We recently moved to Devon, and I explore our transition to a completely different landscape, and some of the wildlife surprises that came with it, towards the end of the book.

In *Close to Home* I consider what might be thought of as the mundane and the everyday but is actually so much more than that. It's about casual or incidental interactions with wildlife on the doorstep, in the garden and in the local countryside, often while doing something else entirely. It's about a sustaining, day-to-day connection with the natural world – and, without wanting to sound melodramatic, it's a significant part of what makes my life feel worthwhile.

In *Human Nature* I take these interactions a step further and explore some of the ideas and issues that develop from everyday experiences. This touches on the conservation of wildlife and some of the more philosophical aspects of the way I have come to think about and value the natural world. I hope some of these thoughts will resonate with others, though, by its very nature, an appreciation of wildlife is a highly personal thing.

The same point comes to the fore in *Conflicts*, where I look at differences in opinions and attitudes that inevitably result in problems in the way we look after our wildlife. Even committed conservationists find it easy to disagree on some of these issues, and I've found myself at odds with friends and colleagues on topics such as the control of Buzzards, introduced species and the extent to which direct human intervention (or interference?) is appropriate when trying to conserve wildlife. And if conservationists struggle to agree, what hope is there of resolving wider conflicts such as the one currently raging between supporters of the beleaguered Hen Harrier and grouse-moor managers?

Finally, *Wild Places* reflects on the increasingly scarce opportunities to escape from places where human influence is all-pervading. It was inspired by the sense of freedom that I appreciate so much, but which is increasingly difficult to come by. Day-to-day interactions with wildlife in an environment dominated by humans are all very well (and all we can hope for most of the time) but every so often I feel the need for more than that. If I can find a wild piece of coastline with no-one in sight, or a fragment of woodland we've been careless enough to 'neglect', and which feels untouched by recent human hands, I relax in a way that is rarely possible in our more obviously modified landscapes.

CLOSE TO HOME

THE ISLAND EFFECT

I've always thought that islands have a magical quality about them. There's something special about the remoteness, the disconnection from 'normal' life on the mainland, reinforced by the need to take a boat to get there. The longer the boat trip the greater the sense of disconnection – and the better the chance of seeing interesting wildlife on the way. I love, too, the way that aspects of wildlife watching are simplified on islands, especially small ones. There may be only a handful of resident birds, and usually just a few more that visit to breed in summer. A bird of any other species simply has to be a migrant on its way to somewhere else. On the mainland things are not so simple. The Swallows I see over the fields by our house in autumn might be local breeders foraging within a few hundred metres of their nest site. Or they might be from nests hundreds of kilometres away, taking a well-earned break on their long journey south.

Islands tend to support far fewer resident birds than similar-sized areas of the mainland. There are good reasons for this. In order to colonise an island, at least two individuals (of opposite sexes) must disperse across a hostile expanse of ocean to get there. And even if a small population becomes established it will be vulnerable to local extinction, from chance events such as severe weather or a period when food is in short supply, and the whole colonisation process must then be repeated.

But what islands lack in resident birds, they more than make up for in their capacity for attracting waifs and strays. Again, this reflects some simple geographical principles. Think of an exhausted migrant flying over the sea and desperately seeking somewhere to rest up and recuperate. There, on the horizon, is a speck of land, the only thing visible other than ocean. Birds home in from all directions, as there are simply no other options available. In contrast, migrants approaching the mainland have a far wider range of options and birds will tend to be more evenly and thinly distributed when they make landfall.

Given my love of islands (and the coast more generally), I'm not quite sure how we ended up living in the flatlands of land-locked Cambridgeshire. I could try to blame my former employers for basing their headquarters in Peterborough. And the inflated house prices on the nearest stretch of coastline in nearby north Norfolk certainly didn't help. Thankfully, we have at least managed to replicate some aspects of the island effect. We live in an old, red-brick farmhouse, sitting isolated in a vast sea of intensive arable farmland. The garden is roughly fifty metres long and forty metres wide, and has plenty of cover provided by twelve mature Sycamore and Horse-chestnut trees, as well as a dense flank of *leylandii* cypresses on three sides and a short section of Hawthorn hedge. The nearest bushes and trees outside the garden are over 400 metres away to the east. Across a great sweep of the view to the west and north a full twenty minutes is required to walk the two kilometres to the next areas of cover. Out there lies nothing but arable crops, crisscrossed by fen ditches and the strips of vole-rich rough grassland that run alongside.

The 'island effect' is very clearly reflected in the birdlife of the garden. There are just ten species that I would regard as residents, birds that breed within the confines of the garden and use it regularly throughout the year: Little Owl, Woodpigeon, Stock Dove, Collared Dove, Dunnock, Robin, Blackbird, Wren, Carrion Crow and Chaffinch. There are, of course, many other frequent visitors, but there are also some notable absentees. For the first two years after we moved in, both House Sparrow and Blue Tit evaded the garden list – this despite my best efforts to attract them by putting out food in winter, and regular sightings of both these birds in the village just over a kilometre away. At first, I was irritated to be missing out on two species that the majority of garden-listers take for granted. Over time, though, I have come to take an almost perverse pleasure in the fact that the garden is so isolated that these common and widespread birds have not managed to reach it. When, in year three, I finally saw a sparrow on one of the bird feeders I was delighted for two reasons. First, it was a new garden tick. More importantly, the distinctive chestnut crown and black patch on the cheek meant that the bird was in fact a Tree Sparrow. The garden was still out of reach for the local House Sparrows, and the 'island effect' remained intact.

As on an offshore island, I enjoy the way that garden birding here is simplified. If I see a recently fledged Wren, Blackbird or Robin then I can be certain that the nest was within the garden even if I failed to notice it. There are simply no other suitable breeding sites for these species within just-fledged-juvenile range.

Migrants also stand out. There are no breeding Chiffchaffs, Willow Warblers or Goldcrests, so each individual I see here can only be a genuine migrant, sucked in from across the landscape by our island of trees. More unexpected migrants have included a stunning male Redstart by the pond one fine May morning. And two weeks later its rarer cousin, the Black Redstart, put in a surprise appearance: a female, flicking her tail nonchalantly from the low roof of an outbuilding – as if she had lived there for years.

Perhaps most intriguing of all are the regular but infrequent visitors. An occasional Rabbit takes up residence in late summer, having survived a perilous journey across the open fields, dodging the local Stoats, Foxes and Buzzards. The same thing has happened on two occasions with lone Grey Squirrels in the autumn, presumably young animals looking to find a secure place to settle down, albeit several kilometres from the nearest woodland. At first these new additions to the garden's wildlife seem strangely incongruous, despite the ubiquity of the species, but we quickly learn to take them for granted. Then, after a few weeks, we realise that we haven't seen them for a while and they must either have moved on or fallen victim to a predator. Who knows how long it might be before the next appearance?

I've seen a party of Long-tailed Tits in the garden on just four occasions. I can't help but speculate about the decision-making of the lead bird in each group. What is it that, just occasionally, makes it turn in this direction and risk a flight of over 400 metres across open country? Is there any 'discussion' between the birds or do they all obligingly follow a chosen leader? Are the birds running short of food in their usual haunts? They seem to find things to eat when they get here, though the fact that they tend not to stay long or return quickly suggests that conditions are not ideal. The paucity of small trees and bushes may help to explain that. I hope that one day I might catch them in the act. It would be too much to expect to chance upon the moment of arrival, but, with patience, perhaps I'll be able to watch them leave – a bouncing string of long-tailed feather-balls heading out across the inhospitable prairie. If they head west or north they'll be well out of binocular range by the time they make 'landfall'.

Postscript

By sheer coincidence, almost as if writing about it had made a difference, a Blue Tit finally appeared in the garden, more than three years after we first moved in. It was soon joined by another and then a third, with two or three seen daily through that autumn and the following winter. In spring they went one better and nested in a hastily erected box. Most of the young died in the nest box (perhaps an indication that the garden was not ideal breeding habitat), but at least two fledged successfully and were a frequent sight on the feeders through the summer. Having found our island, this bird seemed keen to remain on it.

A year or so later, I found evidence in the loft showing that House Sparrows were once in residence too. Numerous gaps in the brickwork of the chimney were stuffed with wads of ancient dried grass, decaying to powder when pulled out for closer inspection. One of these 'fossil' nests held the tiny shrivelled husk of a House Sparrow chick – a reminder of better times for this familiar species, if not for the individual concerned. Perhaps this very nest was the last of the line?

As for the Long-tailed Tits, I never did see them depart the garden and head out across open country. I still watch them regularly in our current garden in Devon, but they leave the feeders, and the garden, by moving methodically along the hedgerow that joins us to the surrounding landscape. We are no longer living on an island.

THE LATE-SUMMER LULL

Ask a sample of birdwatchers about their least favourite time of year and a high proportion will say late summer. Ask them to name their least favourite month and I imagine July and August would emerge as the most frequent choices. In birding circles, late summer is well known as a period of relative inactivity – a time for writing up notes, for family holidays and (if you are so inclined) for looking ahead to the start of the new football season, rather than for spending long hours in the field. Why is this? It's certainly not due to a shortage of birds, as this is the time when bird populations are at their peak. The countryside is awash with new recruits after the breeding season, and before harsh weather and food shortages have taken their toll. Presumably it's not related to the weather, as July and August are our warmest and often driest months – providing some of the most pleasant conditions for being outside.

There are two well-known problems with these months from a birder's perspective. First, despite the high numbers of birds, many are rather inactive and difficult to see. This is the time of the annual moult in many birds, evidenced by their tatty and dishevelled appearance. Take a look at your local Blackbirds, Robins and Magpies for example – three species that can look particularly scruffy at this time of year. Birds tend to moult in late summer to take advantage of the warm conditions, abundant food and the fact that the busy breeding season has drawn to a close. A combination of tatty, worn-out old feathers and part-grown new ones is not ideal for strong flight, and so in order to minimise predation risks, moulting birds tend to keep a low profile. Birds are also rather quiet at this time of year. Songs are no longer needed to attract members of the opposite sex or to hold on to valuable breeding territories. As a result, our farmland, woodlands and gardens become far quieter places, and the birds they support are more difficult to find.

The second problem with July and August is immediately apparent to the twitching element of the birding community – the chasers of the rare and unusual. Late summer is a time when rather few birds are on the move. Our summer migrants have mostly finished breeding, but conditions are benign and they are generally happy to loiter in the breeding areas, finishing their moult and making the most of an abundant food supply. Our wintering birds are doing much the same thing, on their breeding grounds well to the north and east of Britain. At times, nothing very much seems to be happening, and it can be hard to muster that sense of anticipation that comes with setting out on a birding trip at other times of the year. In spring, new migrants are pouring in and we are renewing acquaintances with species that have been absent for many months. In early summer, the breeding season is in full swing and birds in immaculate plumage are filling the air with song. In autumn, huge numbers of migrants are on the move and this is the best season for turning up the unexpected. Even in the depths of winter, birds can be on the move. A spell of cold weather may cause vulnerable species to head south or west to escape the conditions, providing a turnover of birds and the chance of a surprise.

I mentioned the generally good weather that we tend to have in July and August – but actually it's good weather for sunbathing and lounging around rather than for watching birds. Hot conditions result in sluggishness and lethargy in birders as well as in birds. The sun is high overhead for much of the day, the light can be flat and uninspiring (to the annoyance of photographers), and heat haze is often a problem when using a telescope to home in on distant subjects.

I'm writing this in early September, feeling quietly pleased that autumn is finally here and one more of life's late-summer lulls has been safely negotiated. The autumn migrants and winter visitors have yet to materialise in force, but the sense of anticipation is back – the misty early mornings hint at what is to come, even if this promise is, as yet, unfulfilled. But I've also been reflecting on the last two months and thinking that they haven't really been so bad. There have been some notable highlights, including some birding spectacles that are not to be found at any other time of year. I've started to wonder if the late-summer lull is, at least partly, a state of mind rather than a real issue. If you happen to be reading this in late June or early July then I hope the following highlights, based on my last two months in the Cambridgeshire Fens, will offer at least a few crumbs of comfort, despite the lack of anything particularly unusual.

The start of July coincided with peak levels of activity in the Barn Owl box, perched high on its pole just beyond the garden fence. Having had no previous experience of this species near the nest I was amazed at just how active the birds were in daylight. The adults indulged in bouts of feeding in the middle of the day, bringing in several small mammals in quick succession (it was an excellent year for Field Voles). The young were now old enough to take turns appearing at the entrance of the box, turning their heads one way, then the other, to see what was going on. A local ringer visited in the first week of July and confirmed that there were five young, four of a decent size and one much smaller. We had to rescue the 'runt' from the ground several times, and then one day we found its lifeless body below the box, but the four larger birds fledged successfully and were a regular sight in and around the garden through the late summer.

Our Little Owls also had a good breeding season, with at least three young fledged from the usual nest site in one of the garden Sycamores. The owlets would bob up and down on the lip of the hole, in a line of sight just above my computer screen, as if checking to make sure I was still working. They remained a regular sight around the garden once fully fledged, becoming ever more adventurous and independent through the late summer. The previous year, Kestrels had used the same hole, shredding the air with their calls, and bringing in a conveyer-belt of small birds and mammals from the surrounding fields.

July and August are the two key months for harvesting crops in lowland Britain, and that brings a welcome change to the landscape, as well as some enhanced birding opportunities. This year the field surrounding the house was oilseed rape. By mid-July it had all gone, with just bare earth and weedy stubbles remaining. And all at once there were huge numbers of birds on view. Admittedly these were mostly common and familiar species, but they made a refreshing change from staring out at the serried ranks of a dense and birdless crop. There were five species of gull at times, including a lovely adult Mediterranean Gull – a long-anticipated, but very welcome, addition to the house list. Hundreds of Woodpigeons and Stock Doves hoovered up spilt seed and smaller birds included Reed Buntings, Skylarks, family parties of Yellow Wagtails and a regular flock of over 200 Linnets. A handful of Lapwings brought an autumnal feel to the field in August, enhanced by a lone Wheatear, already on its way back south for the winter. Encouraged by this abundance I made an effort to get outside early each day when there was no heat haze to worry about and the light was clear and crisp.

Another feature of the late summer here, almost as predictable as the harvest, is the gathering of hirundines in sizeable flocks. In July and August, Swallows take to roosting in small patches of reeds at the edge of the wide fen drain running close to the house – spooked occasionally by a hunting Marsh Harrier or Sparrowhawk. During the day, they often feed around the garden, always on the leeward side of the trees where flying insects become concentrated. On damp, overcast and breezy days there can be up to fifty Swallows (and a few House Martins) weaving in and out of the garden, sometimes passing within a metre or two of the upstairs windows. A sudden bout of alarm calling and a panicked bunching of the flock has me scanning the skies above. Hunting Hobbies tend to home in on farmsteads and villages out here in the Fens, sensibly concentrating their efforts where potential prey is most abundant.

Having made the case that there are still some birds to be seen in July and August, it's worth remembering that other wildlife is also much in evidence at this time of year. Our Brown Hares become visible once again after the harvest, and the newly independent young of other mammals are busy dispersing and trying to find places to settle. Last July, frantic barking from our easily panicked Cocker Spaniel alerted us to our first garden Hedgehog, and several well-grown Fox cubs were seen regularly just the other side of the fence – eyed suspiciously by our free-roaming hens. Butterflies and dragonflies come into their own in late summer, relishing the hot conditions. In mid-July this year the track leading to the house hosted countless male Black-tailed Skimmers on hot days, rising and quickly re-settling as we walked or drove by.

As in previous years, July and August brought no great rarities and no great excitement to this part of the Fens. But there was more than enough to get me through to the autumn and the promise of better things to come. If July and August really are the dullest months for birders (and, on balance, they probably are), we can take comfort from the fact that they still have so much to offer.

MAN'S BEST FRIEND?

Domestic pets can be a contentious subject among wildlife enthusiasts. Cats take much of the flack. There has been a long-running debate about their potential impact on local bird populations and what, if anything, can be done to reduce it. At least dogs tend not to kill as much wildlife, although, as will become clear, there are exceptions. Unlike cats, however, dogs spend long periods dashing around in the countryside at high speed, forcing wildlife to take rapid evasive action. In sensitive habitats such as beaches with concentrations of terns or waders this disturbance can cause serious problems.

Our current dog is an energetic, enthusiastic and not-very-well-trained Cocker Spaniel. Much of my time in the local countryside serves the dual purpose of watching wildlife and dog walking, two activities that do not always sit comfortably together. Before we go any further, there are some admissions of guilt that I should probably make.

Cocker Spaniels are unbelievably good at tracking down wild-life. They primarily use smell rather than sight, and dense cover or waterlogged vegetation provides no obstacle. The use of a lead helps reduce the potential for mishaps but, unfortunately, offers no guarantees. Thankfully, most animals are adept at getting out of the firing line by flying, running or swimming away. Teazel has two reactions to the occasional creature that is unable to effect an escape or chooses not to try. She jumps back in exaggerated alarm from animals that are big or seem dangerous, such as Mute Swans and Grass Snakes. And she grabs and consumes everything else. Even within the confines of our garden, young birds that leave their nests prematurely put themselves at risk. So far, to the best of my knowledge, nothing very rare has been eaten, and based on the number of Pheasants, Moorhens and Woodpigeons in the area even local populations have been unaffected. But it's not pleasant to witness and, frankly, I'd be annoyed if I came across anyone else's dog behaving in this way. Yet, so far, I've been unable to find a fool-proof way to ensure that mine behaves any better.

I've glossed over the animals that manage to escape predation, and while they might be considered the lucky ones, they still have to expend energy in making their getaway. Especially in cold weather and when food is in short supply, they may not have huge energy reserves at their disposal. If animals are repeatedly disturbed this can quickly deplete reserves and, ultimately, survival rates are reduced. This is particularly true for concentrations of large waterbirds such as wintering swans and geese, for which getting off the ground takes a considerable amount of energy. A single incident can affect hundreds, if not thousands, of birds. In the farmland where we walk I don't think disturbance is much of an issue, but it does still enter my thoughts every time we put up a group of Skylarks or winter finches. And in summer, if birds are flushed from their nests, the eggs or chicks become vulnerable to opportunistic predators, canine or otherwise.

Finally, as well as the effects on wildlife, there are also the impacts on wildlife watching to consider. Animals with any sense either lie low or clear off when a lolloping spaniel appears on the horizon. Using a lead reduces the flushing range but makes holding binoculars almost impossible. Butterfly and dragonfly watching becomes a real problem. Any pause to inspect a settled insect more closely is interpreted as an indication that something edible may have been located, with results that are all too predictable.

Surprisingly, perhaps, there are also some positive aspects to dog ownership when it comes to watching wildlife, though admittedly these are benefits for *me* rather than for the local wildlife. First and foremost, owning a dog gets me out of the house every day, even if it's cold, wet, miserable and I'd rather stay indoors. I always take binoculars. If I were more disciplined I could go birding every day without a dog and see more birds. But I'm naturally inclined to slothfulness and, overall, being a dog owner gets me into the field more often than would otherwise be the case. Regular walks in the same places close to home are the best way to appreciate how much the local wildlife changes from day to day – how changes in crop management are exploited, for example, and just how transient the appearance of some birds can be.

Although the birding opportunities are usually diminished by dog walking, there have been a few memorable exceptions. Just occasionally, Teazel manages to flush something I would not otherwise have seen. Her determined and methodical exploration of a narrow and unpromising field ditch once forced a Jack Snipe out into the open, a species I'd not seen for years. And her cowardly but comical reaction to snakes (dead or alive) has shown just how common Grass Snakes are in the seemingly unpromising arable-dominated landscape around the house. She has found several killed by grass cutting along tracks and byways in the summer, or by the dredging of reeds from the margins of ditches in the autumn. Often, they were hidden beneath piles of cut vegetation, and without her keen and inquisitive nose they would have escaped my attention.

Perhaps the most unexpected benefit of dog ownership has been the regular insights into natural behaviour that come from watching how wild animals respond to a potential predator. There was the time when the lead was jerked out of my hands and Teazel took off in hot pursuit of one of the local Brown Hares. At first I was seriously worried. I'd only recently phoned the police about illegal hare coursing, and now here I was participating in it. But I had no cause for concern. I looked up to see that the hare was already, somehow, on the far side of the field, with the dog trailing hopelessly far behind. I'd seen plenty of running hares before but this was the first time I fully appreciated just how quickly (and effortlessly) they cover the ground.

A few weeks later we inadvertently cornered a hare close to the junction of two fen drains. Again I was concerned, but again it wasn't a problem. The hare nonchalantly flopped into the drain and swam across, leaving a trail through the thin layer of early-winter ice. I didn't know they could do that! And I didn't know that Moorhens could escape predators when taken by surprise by throwing themselves underwater and swimming away unseen. The initial splash and subsequent underwater trail of silt and bubbles are highly suggestive of Water Vole, and without a follow-up sighting I'm not always sure which animal is involved. It's perhaps not surprising that these two species have evolved a similar escape mechanism, given their similar habits; no doubt they regularly face the same potential predators.

Dogs get a bad press with wildlife watchers, and I sympathise with anyone who despairs at the havoc they sometimes cause. I wouldn't want to be without one. But when the time eventually comes, perhaps Teazel will be replaced with a less energetic animal, and a breed with less of a reputation for the relentless tracking down of wildlife.

A RAT'S LIFE

Try as I might (and I really do try) I just can't help but find Brown Rats sinister and menacing. I see them regularly out here in the Fens – rather too regularly for my liking. They often scuttle across local roads in front of the car, particularly in the autumn. I think they are attracted to roadsides at this time of year by spilt grain and other crops, lost overboard from farm trailers in transit from field to silo. Usually it's just the odd one, but once I saw eight together at the edge of the road, scattering in all directions when caught in the car's headlights.

I also see them in the garden, and here too, activity seems to peak in the autumn and early winter. I sometimes almost forget about them in the summer, though on one occasion in late August I inadvertently unearthed a nest of writhing, naked babies from the compost heap. But as autumn progresses and the weather starts to turn cold, I notice increasing signs of activity. Telltale piles of disturbed (and disturbing) dark soil appear, spilling out from under the chicken house and around the edges of the boundary fence. Their well-used runs start to become obvious across the lawn, connecting up strategically important bits of the garden and making it feel as if they are trying to take over – a network of pathways implies a network of rats. Then there is the occasional dropping and frequent signs of feeding activity. I especially notice part-eaten conkers from the Horse-chestnut trees where the rich, shiny-brown surface has been chewed away to reveal the incisor-scarred yellow flesh beneath. Judging by these remains they never seem to eat a whole one, preferring instead to nibble away a small corner before losing interest and moving on to something else. I've found whole piles of them in hidden corners of the garden, each with a small fraction of the nut consumed.

Sightings of the animal itself are patchy but frequent enough. Often I'll catch one in the headlights of the car as I pull up on the drive, or in the beam of the torch when I'm putting the hens to bed or fetching logs from the shed. Periodically, one will be seen in broad daylight, shuffling unapologetically along the edges of a flowerbed or venturing out across the lawn. These diurnal animals are usually wary and alert but occasionally become bolder. One even took to sitting in full view, as bold as brass, on the seed tray of one of the bird feeders.

Logically, I should regard these animals as a welcome addition to the garden's wildlife and enjoy their presence here. We don't get many mammals in the garden, and certainly not ones that can be observed regularly as they go about their business. True, they are an introduced species, but that doesn't stop me appreciating our Little Owls, and Brown Rats have been here in Britain for considerably longer. In some situations rats can cause people real problems. They contaminate food stores with their droppings and urine. And they chew their way through almost anything to gain access to food and shelter, or simply to help wear down their ever-growing rodent incisors. They also carry various unpleasant diseases. Despite this extensive charge sheet, they have caused us no more than the occasional minor inconvenience. Their earth spoil heaps can pile up on the lawn and have to be kicked flat before the grass is cut. They have been known to steal food from the bird feeders (though it's not called stealing when other wildlife takes it), and we have had to invest in secure storage bins for the hen food to prevent rats from gaining access. I'm not worried about catching diseases from them even though it may, technically, be possible. Really, I have no logical reason to resent their presence here.

On reflection, I think my inherent dislike of this animal stems from a lifetime of indoctrination – and serves as a good example of just how powerful this can be. It probably started at school when I learnt about the horrors of the Black Death and the role played by rats and their fleas (another despised creature) in its spread, and has been reinforced constantly since then.* Rats make a regular appearance in films and documentaries as potent symbols of filth and squalor. They are almost universally referred to as 'pests', and any decent garden centre will be stocked full of poisons and traps to help with their control. To convince any doubters, there will be menacing drawings on the boxes, depicting it as a creature that deserves all that it gets.

During periods when the garden population has been particularly high I've felt the need to use lethal control, based solely on my in-built mistrust of the species. I can't bring myself to use

---

* It was the Black Rat, rather than the more recently introduced Brown Rat, that helped spread the plague in Britain. In Central Asia, marmots were apparently responsible for spreading the same disease, making me wonder if they are as despised in that part of the world as rats are here.

poison (the easy option), knowing that it works by preventing the blood from clotting. Death is from internal bleeding and can take several days. Another problem with poison is that any bait accessible to a rat is also available to smaller mammals, and it can lead to accidental poisoning of predators including Barn Owls and Kestrels. Attempts to use a cage trap turned out to be ineffective. In any other creature a rat's ability to sense danger and avoid it would be regarded as a sign of intelligence and draw our admiration. In rats it seems only to highlight just how sneaky and slippery they are. I caught more Blackbirds than rats in the cage trap, when they wandered in to steal the bait. They could be released unharmed but it required constant vigilance to make sure they weren't stuck inside for any length of time. In the end an air rifle proved to be the most effective (and selective) form of rat control – and also, I think, the most humane.

It was only when I started shooting rats that I really began to question my feelings about this animal. Ali, my daughter, was one of the people who challenged me, posing the perfectly reasonable question, 'What have they ever done to you?' I geared myself up to provide an explanation, only to realise that I didn't have one – not a convincing one in any case. I didn't think that harking back to the Black Death would help.

My wife, Hazel, was happy enough that I was shooting them, sharing my instinctive dislike of this animal. And if she had any lingering doubts they disappeared one cold October evening. I was alerted by a piercing scream from the kitchen, sufficiently penetrating to make me glad we had no near neighbours. It was elicited by the sight of a plump rat sitting outside on the window-sill, calmly staring in through the glass. It appeared interested in the feeding opportunities, or perhaps just the warmer conditions, on the other side of the double-glazing. The facial expression seemed to suggest it was trying to work out how to get in. We regularly find Wood Mice in the house but have always been able to catch them with Longworth (live-catch) traps. And despite the odd dropping, a few nibbled cereal boxes and the irritating night-time scrabbling noises, they are such endearing animals that we don't resent the incursions. The idea of a Brown Rat gaining entry was rather less appealing – and the control programme was continued with renewed vigour.

I'm often surprised by the strength of negative feelings some people have towards animals I enjoy watching. Although we lose the odd hen from the garden I wouldn't want to be without the local Foxes. Moles move more soil around than rats, even dest-abilising parts of the lawn with their subterranean pathways, yet I regard the occasional sighting of one above ground as a rare treat rather than anything sinister. Although I understand the reasons why Foxes and Moles are disliked, the level of hostility shown towards them by some people still takes me by surprise. The same is true for moths, bats, Badgers, Cormorants, Grey Herons, Magpies and even birds of prey, all of which are loathed with a vengeance in some quarters. Given my own prejudices, perhaps I should be more understanding of these views. I can imagine a rat enthusiast trying to persuade me to leave these animals alone – and failing, despite the unassailable logic of the argument. No doubt those who don't much like moths, Moles or Foxes would be equally immune to any arguments that I might care to offer in their defence. When it come to our attitudes towards wildlife, sometimes, it seems, logic alone is not enough.

LOCAL PATCH WILDLIFE

'Local patch' is a rather grand description for the farmland within easy walking distance of the house. This is not an area in any way exceptional for wildlife, though it does have a few things in its favour. But it's dominated by the flat, arable farmland that is typical of the Cambridgeshire Fens, with crops of cereals, oilseed rape, sugar beet, potatoes and beans.

One of the main fenland drains, about eight metres wide, passes close to the house – a linear oasis of wetland habitat carved through a bleak desert of farmland. Sedge and Reed Warblers chatter their way through the summer, hidden in the reed-fringed margins. Otters fish this drain, though we are aware of them only through finding their strangely sweet-smelling spraints, glinting with fish scales, along the bank and under road bridges. Like an addict, I feel compelled to pick them up and sniff them each time I find a new sprainting site, more by way of celebration than from any need to confirm the identification. Even Badgers use the drain, building their sett into the bank about 300 metres from the house. With a judiciously positioned telescope (and no little patience) we can watch them from an upstairs window in the early-summer evenings, until the bankside vegetation grows too tall.

There are numerous smaller side drains and ditches, with strips of rough grassland running alongside, offering further variety within the cropped fields. The only mature trees are the Sycamores, Horse-chestnuts and *leylandii* within our garden.

It really is *my* local patch, because despite years of daily visits I've never seen anyone else take the slightest interest in the wildlife here, at least not in a positive way (of which more later). I enjoy being the only person watching this area. It means that when something unusual turns up it will be me that finds it, if anyone does. There is satisfaction in knowing that the birds I see would otherwise not be noticed, which is not always the case when visiting well-watched sites. The wildlife here, as across a large proportion of our wider countryside (away from nature reserves and public spaces), goes largely unseen and unheralded.

On most jaunts around the patch, I see nobody else. Occasionally, if I'm walking on one of the public rights of way, I'll come across a dog walker from the local village. Less often I'll meet a horse rider, or people riding mountain bikes or even motorbikes. Along the main drain I see the occasional fisherman (often from eastern Europe), casting hopeful lines into the water and furtive looks up to the house if successful, all too aware of the peculiar British tradition of wrenching fish from the water only to put them straight back in again. Then there are the local farmers and contractors, usually safely sealed off from the environment inside a four-by-four or the enclosed cab of a tractor. The only other people I've seen include a few hare coursers with their distinctive long dogs and, at night, people out lamping, flooding the blackness with their powerful, rotating beams of light.* The hare coursers and lampers clearly have an interest in the local wildlife, though, like the fishermen, they are really only interested in catching and killing it.

I can't be sure that everyone I see lacks any positive interest in wildlife. Perhaps some of the dog walkers and horse riders are cheered by the song of Skylarks high above them in spring, or the flocks of Lapwing that rise up in great swirling masses in winter. Perhaps the fishermen take at least a casual interest in the Great Crested Grebes, Mute Swans and Tufted Ducks on the drain and, if they are lucky, the occasional Kingfisher or Water Vole. Maybe some of the farm workers enjoy being surrounded by clouds of screeching gulls when they are ploughing the fields, and delight in the Brown Hares fleeing ahead of their machines. But using the 'binocular-carrying test' as a reasonable indicator of keen interest, it really is just me out here actively looking for and enjoying the wildlife.

Steve Dudley, a well-known birder who lives near Peterborough, also has a local patch in the Fens, well away from the nearest nature reserve. He has watched the same area on an almost daily basis for many years. He covers the ground rather more intensively and effectively than I do and has recorded over 150 species of birds. But, with the exception of local birders from Peterborough who visit occasionally specifically to see something rare that Steve has found, he too has never encountered anyone else watching the local wildlife. If he lived elsewhere, these birds would never be found or appreciated by anyone. My patch is near the village

---

* Lamping is a technique used both for legitimate pest control and by poachers. It involves the use of a powerful focused beam of light to illuminate wild animals at night so that they can be killed, usually with a high-powered rifle.

of Gorefield, with about 1,200 residents, and is well served by public access routes. Steve's is only a few kilometres from the 200,000 people living in Peterborough. There must be vast areas of farmland in the Fens, as elsewhere, that is more remote from human settlements and less well served with public access routes. Just how much of the farmed landscape of this country supports birds and other wildlife that no-one ever sees?

Thinking back to my days growing up in the Chilterns, it was much the same story. I spent countless hours in the Beech woods surrounding our house but cannot recall ever seeing anyone else looking for wildlife. These woods supported generations of Nuthatches, Marsh Tits, woodpeckers and other birds that were never seen, or appreciated, by anyone. Only those individuals that strayed into nearby village gardens to take hand-outs would have had any chance of connecting with humanity.

The contrast with high-profile, well-visited, nature reserves is staggering. The RSPB's Titchwell reserve is just over an hour's drive from where I live. Even if you turn up at first light, in the middle of winter, on a weekday, when it's raining, you'll be lucky to have the place to yourself. On a better day, you'll be sharing the reserve with hundreds of other people and will have to fight for a spot in one of the hides. And you'll be very fortunate to see a single bird that has not already been watched by numerous pairs of eyes. To a greater or lesser extent, the same is true of nature reserves around the country. Indeed, many birdwatchers adopt their nearest nature reserve as their favoured local patch rather than choosing somewhere out in the wider countryside.

Does it matter that so much of our wildlife watching is concentrated in small areas set aside specifically for wildlife, and that huge tracts of land outside these reserves are rarely, if ever, visited? I have mixed feelings. If hardly anyone is looking at the wildlife across large parts of the country then it becomes more difficult to make a convincing argument for its conservation. Yet I find it perversely reassuring that there are still vast areas where you can have the place to yourself, make your own discoveries and see things that would otherwise go unnoticed. These areas may not be especially rich in wildlife, and farmed land is likely to be a lot less rich than it was even a few decades ago,* but, as shown by Steve's efforts, they do still support plenty of interesting species.

Returning to my patch, the rough-grass strips alongside the drains are paid for through agri-environment schemes. This is taxpayers' money paid to farmers specifically to encourage wildlife-friendly farming. At the moment it would appear to be just me that is benefiting from the additional wildlife. Although I'm extremely grateful, does this represent good value for money? According to government figures we spend around £3 billion each year in the UK on subsidies to support farming.† This includes funding that pays for specific environmental benefits as well as broader support to help maintain farm incomes. That works out at roughly £100 for every UK taxpayer. Perhaps, then, we are fully entitled to enjoy the wildlife that we see on the farmland around our home.

---

* Estimates from British Trust for Ornithology (BTO) surveys suggest that we have lost around 1 million birds a year, on average, over recent decades, many of these from farmland habitats. For a comprehensive review, see Newton, I. (2017) *Farming and Birds*. Collins, London.

† The precise figures can be obtained from the gov.uk website.

There is a small breeding population of Yellow Wagtails hanging on here. It's one of the birds that most delights me when it returns each spring, and again a few weeks later when the newly fledged young perch, precariously, on top of the wheat stalks. If they disappear in the next few years, as they have done already in many parts of the Fens, I will miss them and mourn their passing. I don't suppose that anyone else will notice.

FAMILIAR SPECIES

Now that I've left my long-term job as an ornithologist with Natural England I feel slightly more comfortable with the admission that I am about to make. We talk about familiar species all the time when referring to species we see regularly. They are instantly recognisable because we see them so often – they are 'familiar' in the same way that a well-known landmark or a television personality is familiar. However, the term also implies that we know a bit about the basic ecology of the species, and it follows that if we see a species often, we will have lots of opportunities to watch it and learn what it gets up to. I like to think that I regularly pause and take the time to watch animals rather than simply noting the identification and moving swiftly on. That's certainly the case with scarcer species that I come across, though perhaps, now I come to think of it, it's not so true for those I see day in, day out. So, as an ornithologist, how 'familiar' am I with our common and widespread birds? To help show just how much I take some species for granted, I've picked a couple of examples. I've deliberately chosen species that, having thought about it for a while, I realise I don't know very well at all.

I see Tufted Ducks all the time. The males are so obvious that they can be picked out on lakes and gravel pits, even when I am whizzing past at high speed on the motorway. In summer they're present in small numbers on the fen drains around our house, and I occasionally see females with broods of young. It's undoubtedly a familiar bird, and yet how much do I really know about this species? I'm obviously aware of the differences between males and females, and I know they get most of their food by diving underwater for it. But, come to think of it, I don't know exactly what it is they're eating. Is it bottom-dwelling invertebrates, mainly snails and bivalves perhaps? I see them on the fen drains mostly in the summer, and in winter they move away to congregate on larger waterbodies – though I'm not really sure why. If the drains remain unfrozen, as they do most winters, do they not provide an adequate supply of food throughout the year? Although I know that Tufted Ducks are common throughout the year in Britain, I couldn't, off the top of my head, say how many breeding pairs we have or how many thousands come here for the winter, and I'm not sure where all the winter immigrants originate from.

As a conservationist I'm particularly interested in population trends, and I'm aware that Tufted Ducks have increased in recent decades – but I'm not sure by how much or for how long they have been increasing. On large waterbodies in this area, I often see Tufted Ducks in close proximity to Pochards, another diving duck. These two birds look very different and birdwatchers think of them as very different species. Yet, having embarked on this exercise, I realise I would struggle to describe how they differ from each other ecologically, even at the most basic level.

The Coal Tit is a very different bird, though it's also one that almost every birdwatcher would describe as 'familiar'. It's seen regularly at most garden feeders, especially if there is woodland nearby. Away from feeders it tends not to be encountered so frequently, or at least not in situations where it is easy to watch for any length of time. I can't remember the last time I let my binoculars linger on a Coal Tit long enough to find out what it did next. The very act of looking at one through binoculars is usually solely an attempt to make sure that it isn't something else – something, dare I say it, a little more interesting. I could have a stab at summarising some key differences between the ecology of this bird and the similar-sized Blue Tit, but I doubt if I would do a very convincing job.

I've just looked up some basic facts about the Coat Tit's diet and breeding behaviour, much of which was new to me.* I now know (though I will soon forget) that they nest in cavities that are usually at, or close to, ground level, including the burrows of small mammals. They also apparently breed in the base of the stick nests of larger birds. I don't think I've ever seen one at a nest site, despite having spent plenty of time in the breeding season in places where they are common, and the fact that they must make hundreds of visits when bringing food for their young. I've also learnt that Coal Tits are well adapted to search out invertebrates from the tiniest of nooks and crannies high up in the woodland canopy. They are more agile than other tits and more able to manoeuvre themselves into positions where they can exploit such resources. I think I already knew that they take seeds from cones and store them in periods of plenty, though I

---

* I referred to the species account in Snow, D. W. and Perrins, C. M. (1998) *The Birds of the Western Palearctic, Concise Edition*, Volume 2. Oxford University Press, Oxford.

didn't fully appreciate just how important this behaviour is in helping the bird to survive the winter in coniferous forests. Come to think of it, when I see them at a bird feeder their visits are often fleeting; they nip in to steal away a nut or seed rather than lingering with the more abundant Blue and Great Tits.

All of us interested in wildlife constantly make choices about how much time to spend identifying a species and how much to devote to watching its behaviour. Most of us do plenty of both at different times, but there are also extremes at both ends of the spectrum. There are the keen listers whose priority is simply to see and identify as many species as possible. Time spent watching what an animal does is time that could have been better spent looking for a different animal. In contrast, some people devote the majority of their lives to finding out as much as they can about a single species, or a select handful of species. There are researchers who have become world authorities on their chosen study species but who would struggle to identify the common plants and animals in their garden. Which of these two extremes produces the most useful information? Actually, I think it's rather a happy marriage. The 'listers' provide information on the distribution and abundance of animals, which, over time, reveals how populations are changing. The 'researchers' are better at finding out exactly why a species is doing well or badly and, in the latter case, what could be done to try to restore its fortunes. To build a coherent conservation strategy we need plenty of both types of information.

I have shelves full of bird monographs in my study – each one a summary of what is known about a particular species. It's my favourite category of bird book. For me, these volumes get to the very heart of what makes an interest in wildlife so rewarding. What makes each species tick? What sets it apart from other similar species? How is it faring in the modern world and what are its prospects as the world continues to change? Hopefully, soon, someone will write a full-length book about the Coal Tit. And perhaps someone else could take on the Tufted Duck and the Pochard.

There is only one species I feel confident in saying I'm familiar with, and ironically it's one I don't see every day. I know this species well because I have been involved in its reintroduction and have spent thousands of hours watching and studying it in the field. In a way, having a good understanding of this bird, the Red Kite, serves only to highlight the extent of the knowledge gaps for all the other species I see regularly. I aspire to tilt my own personal balance a little more towards the 'research' end of the wildlife-watching spectrum, and I think I should start by learning more about the species I regard as familiar in the local landscape.

ALL-TIME FAVOURITE

I've been asked many times over the years about my favourite bird. As with the same question about books, films or albums, I've always struggled to come up with a consistent answer. When my kids were younger, they went through a phase of persistent interrogation, trying to pin me down, unable to believe that I didn't have a favourite. I realised it would save some time if the matter could be resolved, once and for all.

First, I needed a few ground rules, the absence of which had caused problems in the past. It would need to be a common, widespread and familiar species on the grounds that with rare or localised birds, the answer would inevitably be influenced by recent experiences. A few summers ago, Puffin would have been a contender after a family visit to Hermaness at the northern tip of Shetland. As we sat at the edge of the colony, the birds strutted around our rucksacks while we marvelled at their diminutive size (always surprising for first-time viewers) and comical behaviour. It was the favourite bird for all of us over the next few weeks.

I don't chase after rarities these days but I do enjoy seeing our scarcer species – birds that are known well enough from field guides and birding magazines, but scarce, or tricky to see. It's a long list but it would include birds such as Long-tailed Skua, Jack Snipe, Long-eared Owl, Rough-legged Buzzard, Waxwing, Great Grey Shrike and Shore Lark. If any one of these birds eludes you for a long time in your formative birding years, it makes a real impression when you do finally manage to connect with it. Each one of these birds would have qualified as a favourite for me at one time or another.

Having established the rule that it must be common, widespread and familiar, I was surprised just how quickly the answer came to me. My favourite bird is at the very top of the pile for the first two of these requirements. At the last count there were almost ten million pairs of Wrens in Britain, comfortably eclipsing its closest rivals the Woodpigeon, Robin, Blackbird, Chaffinch and House Sparrow.* Ten million might sound like a lot, but there are roughly seven people in Britain for every pair of Wrens, so they are no real threat to our dominance. Like humans, Wrens occupy an incredibly diverse range of habitats from the highest mountain tops right down to the rocky, windswept coasts of our remotest islands. This is a bird that almost transcends the notion of habitat selection. It can thrive virtually anywhere provided that there is some small-scale structure to the environment in which it can hide away and explore nooks and crannies, seeking out small invertebrates.

Despite its abundance and ubiquity, it is well short of top spot when it comes to familiarity, the third of my qualifying criteria. That's partly because it's so tiny. It is almost our smallest bird,

* Woodward, I., Aebischer, N., Burnell, D. *et al.* (2020) Population estimates of birds in Great Britain and the United Kingdom. *British Birds* 113: 69–104.

pipped at the post only by the diminutive Goldcrest and Firecrest. Mark Cocker pointed out that it also has the joint smallest name of any British bird, sharing the title with Knot, Ruff, Smew and Rook, among others, although he cheated with Jay by including the prefix 'Eurasian'.* The Wren's rufous-brown plumage is intricately and delicately patterned in close-up but rather nondescript and drab when seen from a distance, and that also helps it to keep a low profile. And it is surprisingly unobtrusive in its behaviour. Although it's a very active bird, constantly on the move, it tends to keep close to, or within, cover and is rarely out in the open for long. At times, it resorts to creeping and scuttling around obstacles rather than flying, and at first glance it can easily be mistaken for a small mammal. Conor Jameson called it 'the underworld bird' for its furtive behaviour.† It is often given away by its song, which is incredibly loud for such a small creature and seems rather out of character for a bird that is otherwise so unobtrusive. It is one of the few British birds that sings throughout the year. Along with the Robin it maintains a territory through the winter, periodically shattering the silence with explosive bursts of song.

The Wren makes full use of human structures and artefacts throughout the year. In our garden I regularly watch one foraging along the walls of the house, working along the undersides of window ledges and gutters where invertebrates seek refuge. I have watched one disappearing into the wheel arch of our car parked on the drive and, every so often, one has to be coaxed

---

* Cocker, M. and Mabey, R. (2005) *Birds Britannica*. Chatto & Windus, London.

† Jameson, C. M. (2014) *Shrewdunnit: The Nature Files*. Pelagic Publishing, Exeter.

out of the garage, having entered through an open window or a door left ajar. In cold conditions, Wrens gather together overnight to help conserve heat, and up to forty or fifty birds have been found huddled within a nest box. In the spring it will breed using open-fronted nest boxes, and indeed it is famous for appropriating all manner of human objects for its nest site. The account in *Birds Britannica* lists, among others, the mouth of a dead Pike hanging on a garage wall, a scarecrow's pocket, the folds of a church curtain, an old hat in a busy workshop and a site within twenty centimetres of an industrial circular saw in regular use.* One reason the delightful domed nests are so well known is that the male builds several, seeking to demonstrate his prowess to a prospective mate. If successful, he will leave it to her to decide which nest to line with feathers, ready to receive its clutch of eggs.

Rearing young close to a circular saw in a busy workshop sums up something about this bird I particularly admire, albeit something that means it tends to lose out in overall popularity to other garden birds such as the Robin, Song Thrush, Blackbird and Blue Tit. While it is perfectly happy to exploit opportunities provided by humanity, the bird remains utterly indifferent to humans. Wrens rarely take our hand-outs of food, though occasionally they forage for crumbs on the ground beneath the bird table. And in typical style, Wrens sometimes explore the undersides of bird tables, taking spiders and other invertebrates, while stoically ignoring the food provided above. It is rare to hear of a Wren being tamed in the way that often happens with garden

---

* Cocker and Mabey (2005).

Robins and city House Sparrows. In fact, it is hard to elicit any sort of reaction or acknowledgement from this bird. A Wren is unlikely to fly away when approached closely, although it may quickly duck into cover to continue its relentless quest for food. Wrens live all around our homes and gardens and yet are all but oblivious to us, and I can't help but admire them for that.

Favourite birds, much like favourite albums and football teams, are not always successfully handed down from one generation to the next. However, I'm pleased to say that my son Ben is a fervent (and already long-suffering) Liverpool supporter. And my daughter Ali has most definitely adopted the Wren as her favourite bird. It may have taken me more than fifty years to make a decision, but being able to pass it on to a fellow enthusiast has made the effort well worthwhile.

HUMAN NATURE

NUMBER CONUNDRUM

As a committed conservationist I've long been troubled by the inverse relationship between the abundance of a species and the pleasure that comes from seeing it. In any given place, the scarcer a species might be, the greater the pleasure derived from successfully tracking it down. Before offering examples, I should perhaps explain why exactly this bothers me. Conservationists try to prevent population declines and, where possible, encourage increases. I'm not always convinced that we do this for the sake of the species themselves. The startling loss of farmland birds from our landscapes is not a problem per se for the Yellow Wagtails, Turtle Doves, Skylarks, Linnets and Corn Buntings involved. Those individuals lucky enough to scratch out a living on our intensively managed modern farms are blissfully unaware that they are now fewer in number. But if farmland birds decline then the countryside as a whole is impoverished and there are fewer opportunities for people to enjoy watching wildlife that was once taken for granted. That, in itself, is one of the most powerful arguments for striving to avoid further losses. But does it hold true if we automatically and subconsciously compensate for the declines in certain species by gaining more pleasure from seeing them?

In idle moments I've even pondered on the mathematical nature of the relationship. Might it be linear? If a population declines to 10 per cent of its former levels and is seen ten times less often, does it give us ten times more pleasure each time we manage to see it? I'm not sure, and, thankfully, such subjective assessments would be nigh on impossible to undertake.

Many of our once common and familiar farmland birds have been in free fall. Quite a few have declined by over 50 per cent in a few decades, and a handful of species have declined by more than 90 per cent. Birds like the Grey Partridge, Tree Sparrow, Corn Bunting and Turtle Dove are now scarce or absent in many areas. In the Cambridgeshire Fens, they have become so scarce that just one individual of any of these species is enough to enhance an afternoon's birding. I now take great pleasure from the infrequent sightings of birds that were once a familiar sight and were surely taken for granted by birdwatchers only a generation ago.

We also adjust our levels of appreciation for species whose fortunes have changed for the better. The first few colonising Collared Doves to make landfall on the east coast back in the 1950s attracted visiting birders from across the country. As they spread out, the initial pioneers in each area were greeted with interest and enthusiasm, as a welcome new addition to the local avifauna. A few decades on and I can't think of a bird that is less appreciated by the average birdwatcher. This extends to the song, which is routinely described as 'monotonous', though surely that also applies to the more highly appreciated Cuckoo with which it is sometimes confused. In 1959 the cachet of rarity was still intact, and the eminent ornithologist David Bannerman described the Collared Dove's song as a 'pleasant tri-syllabic *coo coo-coo*'.* Nowadays we are more likely to speak fondly of the *turrrr, turrrr, turrrr* song of the rapidly declining Turtle Dove, a sound that is undeniably monotonous yet much appreciated by those fortunate enough to hear it. If the stories of these two birds were switched, would we also switch our perceptions of the noise they make? I'm convinced that we would.

It's hardly surprising if our responses to birds, and other species, are influenced in this way. It reflects a basic characteristic of human nature. For good reasons we have evolved to pay particular attention to things that are rare and so more difficult to attain in our local environment. It makes good sense, from an evolutionary perspective, to take common things for granted and to seek out the unusual. Mark Cocker summed it up neatly when discussing birds, pointing out that 'a preoccupation with the exceptional is almost hard-wired into the human imagination'.†

It is impossible to quantify, but I'd be surprised if modern naturalists derive any less pleasure from an average day in the field than their counterparts of 100 or 200 years ago, despite the huge declines in wildlife over that period. While I would not, for one minute, suggest conservationists should throw in the towel, I can't help but find it all rather unsettling. We urgently need to protect the natural environment for the essential services it provides, including clean air and water, healthy soils, food, and flood protection. Surely, we should also look after the wildlife that we have left for the sheer joy that it brings us in a world

---

* Cocker, M. and Mabey, R. (2005) *Birds Britannica*. Chatto & Windus, London.
† Cocker, M. (2014) *Claxton: Field Notes from a Small Planet*. Jonathan Cape, London.

increasingly dominated by humanity. That may seem obvious, and yet our highly developed, in-built capacity to adjust expectations as wildlife continues to decline all around us makes it surprisingly difficult to achieve. If there is a lesson to be learnt here it's that we should try to better appreciate what we have now, even the familiar species that we see in large numbers day in, day out. It may not always be thus. In that spirit I will strive to take more pleasure from the hordes of Woodpigeons that flood onto the arable fields around the house. And from the Collared Doves that coo incessantly from the garden.

MARIO OR MUD PIES?

The National Trust runs a campaign headed *Fifty things to do before you are 11¾*. My two children were already into their teens when we first became aware of it, but we did read through the list and found that three of the fifty things had so far eluded them. They had yet to canoe down a river, though we had been on various other types of boat which we thought should probably count. They had not yet learnt to ride a horse. And, as far as we could recall, we had never made mud pies. I say 'we' because that's how it is with outdoor activities these days. The dangers from increased traffic and the perception that ill-intentioned strangers lurk behind every bush mean that children spend their time outdoors under close supervision (if they spend time there at all). I often wonder if that is a good or a bad thing overall. On the positive side it means more time spent together as a family with more opportunities for knowledge and ideas to be passed on, from one generation to the next. But it also means less time for unsupervised exploration and the benefits that brings in encouraging free-thinking and independence. Of greater concern is the fact that many children today spend hardly any time at all outside, through lack of opportunity, and because of the draw of competing interests on the other side of the front door.*

Supervised or not, getting children outside is certainly a battle these days. Henry David Thoreau in his famous book *Walden* cautioned that 'staying in the house breeds a sort of insanity always'.† If that was true in the mid-nineteenth century then it's easy to see why mental wellbeing is so often in the headlines now. The trend of becoming increasingly detached from the natural world has continued at a relentless pace over the last few decades. If, like me, you're in your fifties or older, it's likely you have fond childhood memories of roaming the countryside. Perhaps you collected birds' eggs, or butterflies, or pressed wild flowers. You probably learnt the names of the most common and familiar species, and you probably still know them now. If you are in your twenties or thirties it is less likely you will have these memories.

The *Oxford Junior Dictionary* is regularly updated to reflect the changing times in which we live. Recent updates will help our children cope with modern life, with additions such as 'blog', 'broadband', 'cut-and-paste' and 'celebrity'. But the loss of words relating to the natural world has been widely lamented. Basic words such as 'acorn', 'blackberry', 'buttercup', 'chestnut', 'magpie' and a host of others, all describing familiar sights in the countryside, are now missing – they are no longer deemed to be words that every seven-year-old should know.‡ You can hardly blame

---

* Barkham, P. (2020) Rewilding childhood. *British Wildlife* 31: 265–269.

† Thoreau, H. D. (1854) *Walden; or, Life in the Woods.* Ticknor & Fields, Boston, MA. New edition by Penguin Books, London, 2016.

‡ Robert Macfarlane and Jackie Morris offer a passionate defence of such words in their beautifully illustrated book *The Lost Words: A Spell Book.* Hamish Hamilton, London, 2017.

the editors. For many of our children these words have become wholly irrelevant, because they live in urban areas and are not allowed to play outdoors. They are denied what world-renowned American biologist E. O. Wilson referred to as 'biophilia', something he defined as the 'rich natural pleasure that comes from being surrounded by living organisms'.*

If children don't interact with wildlife as they are growing up then it's unlikely they will do so as adults, or encourage their own children to explore outdoors. Rather than being connected to the natural world in the local woods and fields, kids now are connected, through technology, to the rest of humanity. The average person apparently checks their smartphone every twelve minutes on average and spends three to four hours in front of the TV every day. We track world events in close to real time and can't help but dwell on things that are entirely beyond our control. Increasingly, studies suggest that the more time we spend shackled to modern technology, digitally connecting ourselves to other people's lives, the unhappier we become. Studies also show that interacting with the natural world is good, perhaps essential, for our wellbeing and health; it is what are brains were designed to do. Yet we seem to be swapping one for the other and increasingly losing our way.

To return to my experience as a parent, I've noticed that while it's devilishly hard to persuade kids to go outdoors, once there they almost always have fun. After a few hours exploring a local wood they are glowing, lively, cheerful and full of conversation

* Wilson, E. O. (1990) *Biophilia: The Human Bond with Other Species.* Harvard University Press, Cambridge, MA.

and ideas. After a session helping Mario explore one of his virtual worlds their eyes have glazed over and it's tricky to elicit any kind of response. Yet, when given the option, they always choose Mario. It's much the same with adults, I suppose. The activities that provide us with the most satisfaction take a bit of effort. We are tempted to slump in front of the TV on a Saturday afternoon rather than get out into the garden to dig over the vegetable patch. At times, the temptation is too great and the telly wins. But, as adults, we know from experience that we must force ourselves out of our laziness in order to achieve greater happiness. Young children have yet to learn that, and tend to take the easiest option if they are given the chance.

I struggle to remember whether I needed encouragement to get outside as a child. I think not, though in those days there were fewer competing interests. Kids were perhaps forced outdoors to stave off boredom. Today, children clearly do need to be encouraged and cajoled out of the house and into the local countryside. And if that doesn't work, they should be dragged outside, even if it's cold, wet and windy, and they don't want to go. They may not thank you for it. But it will help ensure that kids in generations to come are still ticking things off the National Trust's 'fifty things' list, and still learning to love the countryside and the wildlife that depends on it.

SPLITTING HEADACHES

Is more information always a good thing? I suppose it is, though sometimes it comes with significant drawbacks, especially if you are comfortable with the status quo. I'm not a great chaser of rarities, but until recently I knew all the names of the birds that turned up regularly in Europe. I now have to think twice when browsing my European field guides. What is a Yelkouan Shearwater, a Maghreb Wheatear or a Turkestan Shrike? I can just about work it out but I slightly resent the effort required to do so. The term 'splitting' seems very apt, describing as it does the division of one species into two or more new ones, as well as the resulting effects on the human head. Keen birders may welcome the increasing number of potential ticks, but the plethora of new species takes some keeping up with.

Adding to the confusion are changes that have nothing to do with splitting but reflect attempts to standardise English names so they can be used throughout the world. Some books aimed at a British readership now refer to Parasitic Jaeger instead of Arctic Skua and Yellow-billed Loon rather than White-billed Diver, resulting from the adoption of the American names for these birds. It's mildly irritating that we have different words to describe the same birds on each side of the Atlantic, but it beggars belief that we can't even agree on the bill colour!

Even the supposedly stable scientific names are prone to sudden and unexpected changes. The generic name *Parus* once covered all our common tits with the exception of Long-tailed Tit. The familiar Blue Tit, for example, was *Parus caeruleus*. The same group of British birds is now covered by a bewildering variety of generic names including *Periparus* (for Coal Tit), *Cyanistes* (Blue Tit), *Lophophanes* (Crested Tit) and *Poecile* (Marsh and Willow Tits). Among European birds, only the Great Tit (*Parus major*) keeps alive the old and familiar generic name. At my age, is it even worth trying to keep track of such extensive changes?

As if new species and new names weren't enough to contend with, the order of species in field guides is in a constant state of flux. The divers and grebes were *always* at the beginning of the book when I was growing up, but no longer. In the guide I consult most frequently the Mute Swan now has the honour of appearing first, perhaps befitting this most royal of birds. The divers and grebes now sit incongruously between gamebirds and shearwaters. This constant re-ordering means that I'm increasingly forced into using the index to locate a particular bird, something that keen birders have long prided themselves in being able to manage without.

The majority of these changes result from the ever-increasing number of genetic studies of birds. Taxonomy was previously based on the relatively crude assessment of morphological and behavioural characteristics of birds. The hawks were grouped together with the falcons as 'birds of prey' because they both have strong hooked beaks and sharp claws, a similar body shape, and they both feed mainly on smaller birds or mammals caught using speed or stealth. Now, these assessments are more often based on DNA from blood or feather samples and, as technology has advanced, so the number of studies undertaken has increased exponentially. DNA can reveal substantial differences between groups of birds that, to the human eye, look similar and behave in a similar way, hence the increasing number of splits, and the dramatic rearrangements in the order of birds in our field guides. The good news (I suppose) is that this is transforming our understanding of the relationships between different birds, correcting previous false assumptions under which we have laboured for decades. The bad news is that it is devilishly difficult to keep up with all the changes.

There is no point resenting all these changes. In the end we have no real choice other than to embrace them and try to learn from them. A recent issue of the journal *British Birds* is a case in point. I thought I'd noticed an error when the 'recent reports' section listed Red-footed Falcon between European Roller and Lesser Grey Shrike, rather than with the other birds of prey. There was no mistake. Recent genetic work has indeed shown that falcons are more closely related to parrots than they are to other raptors. Once I'd got over my initial surprise it started to make sense. Falcons and parrots often nest in tree holes and they both lay their eggs onto the bare substrate rather than constructing a nest. Parrots have strong, pointed, rather raptorial beaks. And they have long, sharply pointed wings allowing for rapid, manoeuvrable flight. There is something rather pleasing in the revelation that a Kestrel is a raptor-shaped parrot that has turned to killing small mammals and birds for sustenance rather than breaking open nuts and fruits. I will never think of them in quite the same way again. Having to learn a few new names and resorting to the index of field guides is perhaps a small price to pay for such interesting advances in understanding.

THE NAMING GAME

I found an Old Lady sleeping in our porch the other morning. You may well groan at the joke, but it worked a treat when I shouted it up the stairs to Hazel. Without the clue from the capital letters, it took her a while to cotton on to the truth. The fact that there was genuine excitement in my voice no doubt helped in the deception – after all, this was a new moth for the garden.

The name for this large moth comes from the dark-patterned wings, which are said to resemble a type of shawl once favoured by ladies of advancing years. Many of our moths have similarly delightful and evocative English names that capture something of the essence of their appearance or behaviour. The Mouse Moth is indeed mousey brown, but the name derives from its distinctive behaviour. When trying to evade capture it scuttles erratically towards cover rather than taking flight. The Hummingbird Hawk-moth really does look and behave like a hummingbird, so much so that it is sometimes mistaken for an exotic escapee. The Elephant Hawk-moth is larger (of course), with bright pink colours predominating, though it is not named after the proverbial pink elephant. Rather, it is the huge larva, reminiscent of an elephant's trunk, that gives it its name. It routinely alarms people when found on garden fuchsias or willowherbs, as it can be mistaken for a small, large-eyed snake, likely gaining protection from birds as a result. Then there is the Maiden's Blush, the Chinese Character, the Scallop Shell, the Lobster Moth and the Peach Blossom, among many other moths with characterful names.*

There are also some charming and evocative plant names, although, in contrast to moths, they seem to be the exception rather than the rule. I'm especially fond of Fox-and-cubs, the dandelion-relative with a cluster of rufous-brown flowers, often with one in full flower (the 'fox') while the nearby 'cubs' are still in bud. The name for Bristly Oxtongue also serves both to denote the species and as a vivid description of a key part of the plant – in this case the distinctive rough, pimply leaves.

Perhaps it's just because I'm more familiar with them, but birds seem to lack such imaginative names. True, many of them are helpful enough. The Barn Owl really does breed in old farm buildings, the Turnstone uses its short, pointed bill to search under pebbles for invertebrates, and the Spoonbill, Redwing, Firecrest, Long-tailed Tit, Treecreeper and many others have sensible and appropriate names. Overall, though, I think bird-watchers have been rather short-changed in comparison with moth enthusiasts. By way of compensation, some of the traditional, or folk, bird names are rather more imaginative, even if

---

* For more moth names and a scholarly but accessible account of their origins (spanning several centuries) see Marren, P. (1998) The English names of moths. *British Wildlife* 10: 29–38; and Marren, P. (2019) *Emperors, Admirals and Chimney Sweepers: The Weird and Wonderful Names of Butterflies and Moths.* Little Toller, Toller Fratrum.

most have faded from everyday use. They are now largely confined to specialist books on the subject or wheeled out to help add colour to a conservation press release. To pick just a few of my favourites, how about Goggle-eyed Plover for Stone-curlew, Butterbump for Bittern (based on its high fat content), Bumbarrel for Long-tailed Tit (from the distinctive shape of the nest) and Seven-coloured Linnet for Goldfinch (which works if you include beak and legs in your calculation).*

A few traditional names have managed to cling on into modern times. My dad still refers to Green Plovers, or Peewits, rather than Lapwings, Dabchicks instead of Little Grebes and English rather than Grey Partridges, all names that are still widely understood, if little used these days, by birdwatchers. The same applies to Yaffle for Green Woodpecker (after its laughing call), Storm Cock for Mistle Thrush (because it sings through the winter) and Windhover for Kestrel (for hopefully obvious reasons). Bonxie and Tystie are commonly used for Great Skua and Black Guillemot respectively, based on traditional names originating in Shetland in the far north, but increasingly adopted by birdwatchers more widely. The Shetland name for Fulmar is the now little-used Maali, though when my young children were visiting the islands they called them 'Flemmers', based on a combination of mishearing me and being warned that the bird could spit foul-smelling oil if you strayed too close to its nest.

Other sections of society also have their own traditional names. I think many people will be familiar with the alternative name

---

* Greenoak, F. (1997) *British Birds: Their Folklore, Names and Literature.* Christopher Helm, London.

of Reynard for Fox, but perhaps not Charlie, widely used by gamekeepers and field sports enthusiasts, apparently after a well-known eighteenth-century hunter. Black-cock or Black-game tend to be used by shooting enthusiasts for Black Grouse, and Frenchman is used by the same group for the introduced Red-legged Partridge, offering an appropriate contrast with the English Partridge.

If the English bird names in current widespread use lack imagination we are, nevertheless, still very attached to them. The various attempts over the years to produce standardised, inter-national English names for birds have not been well received, at least among casual birdwatchers. It was proposed that the Dunnock (or Hedge Sparrow) should be renamed Hedge Accentor to reflect its taxonomic affinities. Bearded Tit suffered a similar fate. It is not a member of the tit family, so the new recommendation was Bearded Reedling. Swallow, we were told, must become Barn Swallow to ensure we don't muddle it up with any of the other swallows, something that makes sense in other parts of the world but is hardly necessary in a British context. These new names have been adopted by publishers of journals and books to a greater or lesser extent but have been largely shunned by birdwatchers. Try sneaking Barn Swallow or Bearded Reedling into casual conversation and you are likely to receive bemused or disdainful looks.

All our British birds, mammals, amphibians, reptiles, flowering plants, butterflies and dragonflies have English or 'common' names. Many of our fungi, moths and other common invertebrates also have them, though by no means all. Scan down any formal inventory of threatened and declining species, and under the column headed 'English name' you will find numerous entries for 'a fly', 'a beetle' or 'a bee', together with the relevant scientific name. Lichens are especially poorly served in this regard. It hardly inspires enthusiasm for a threatened species when it doesn't even exist in the English language, something that has been acknowledged in recent years. More and more species have been dragged into the limelight with the allocation of shiny new English names, including some derived from entries submitted to public naming competitions. Thanks to such innovation we now have Sea Piglet (for a water shrimp), Wannabee Fly (for a hoverfly disguised as a bumblebee) and the formidable sounding Solar-powered Sea Slug. Even the unloved lichens get a look in. The hitherto off-putting *Peltigera venosa* can now be referred to as Pixie Gowns Lichen and *Usnea florida* can enter polite conversation as Witches' Whiskers. Will these names catch on? Hopefully, given time, though for the rarer species the first requirement is to make sure they remain with us for long enough for that to happen.

MISSING FROM THE LIST

Most of us who have an interest in wildlife make lists of one kind or another of the species we've seen. It satisfies our instinct for 'collecting' things and, as with most forms of collecting, it tends to be more prevalent in men than women (though see below for a notable exception). Listing sometimes has a bad reputation, especially when taken to extremes by the 'twitching' element of the birding community. Is it really worthwhile expending so much time and energy (and carbon) travelling great distances in the hope of catching up with a new bird? Does it add anything to the conservation effort?

At the less extreme end of the spectrum, most birdwatchers will have at least one carefully maintained list. Many have several. There is the British list, the world list, the local patch list, the garden list and even the office list. Then there is the year list, to get around the problem of having seen most of the birds in an area. This one can be started afresh, and with renewed vigour, on the first day of January every year.

Any listing exercise requires strict rules about what can and can't be counted. And with rules comes the potential for farce. Take the garden list, for example. This usually includes birds seen *from* the garden (or house) rather than requiring that they land within it. So, if a bird is seen in flight when you're in the garden, you can count it. With modern telescopes, larger and more distinctive birds can be seen and identified from a considerable distance. When we lived two kilometres away from the Ouse Washes reserve close to the Cambridgeshire/Norfolk border I remember casually 'scoping the distant flood-defence bank from the bottom of the garden. Unexpectedly, a flock of birds flew up and, as they briefly appeared above the top of the bank, Black-tailed Godwit was duly added to the garden list.

The same rule also leads to a tricky situation if you see something when you are close to your garden, but not quite home. Some birders take a laid-back view: if it would have been possible to see a bird had you been back in the garden then you can count it. Others are sticklers and so must sprint back home to make sure they actually see the bird from within the property boundary. I'll admit to quickening my pace at the end of a dog walk a few years ago to make sure the first Red Kite I'd seen locally was still in view when I arrived back at the front gate. Keen year-listers face a similarly farcical dilemma if a rare bird turns up near the end of the year. When to go and see it? If they go in late December, they may feel obliged to repeat the journey a few days later.

Listing may seem pointless, and if it comes to dominate all other aspects of an interest in wildlife then something is probably lacking. I went through a twitching phase for a few years, inspired (if that's the right word) by the exploits of other members of the University of East Anglia's bird club. It seems crazy to have spent so many hours in the back of a minibus or a cramped hire car simply to add one new bird to a list. Looking back, if there's a positive aspect to those trips it's not the new birds I managed to see but the new places it took me to. For someone who had grown up in landlocked Oxfordshire, visiting the Isles of Scilly, Orkney and other far-flung sites for the first time was a revelation, even if there was limited time to enjoy them before we had to head home.

I still have a fondness for species lists (not just birds), even if I'm no longer prepared to travel great distances to add to them. And despite their apparent futility, and the bad press they attract, I think there are some very good reasons for keeping lists, both on an individual level and for the potential contribution to wider knowledge. It's enjoyable and it helps to add a competitive edge to an interest in wildlife. It allows comparisons, not only between individual birders, but also between different areas. I've moved house seven times in my adult life, and one of the first things I think about when settling into a new house is whether the garden, or local patch, lists will exceed those of previous homes.

Whenever I go abroad, even if it's just for a few days, I always note down the birds seen and tot them up at the end of the trip. The figure can be surprisingly low. I managed just twenty-nine species on a family skiing trip to Bulgaria, where there was little time for birding. Most were seen from the coach between the airport and the mountains, pottering around the hotel in early morning, and on the daily minibus trips between the hotel and the ski slopes. This kind of casual listing serves no real purpose other than helping to pass the time. We are programmed to strive for meaning in almost everything we do, but we shouldn't underplay the value of relaxation and enjoyment, pure and simple, when it comes to watching wildlife and reflecting on what we have seen.

Of course, if something is enjoyable then it helps keep the mind focused and means we are more likely to maintain our interest. Keen patch-listers often develop an encyclopaedic knowledge of the birds in their area. They know the species they have seen on their patch, the species they have yet to see but which have been seen by others (the stuff of nightmares), as well as those that have been seen in the wider area and so might be expected to turn up given time. They are driven to put in the hours because that reduces the chance of missing something that could drop in for a short time and not reappear for several years.

Whether all this knowledge and recording effort ends up being put to good use depends on the individual, but it certainly can be. Traditionally, bird records were submitted to the local country recorder and, when combined with the observations of others, contributed to building up an understanding of bird distribution and (over time) population trends. That route is still open, but in recent years national recording schemes have also been developed. The British Trust for Ornithology's BirdTrack encourages the submission of records online and can provide surprisingly detailed information about patterns of movements and distribution when information from thousands of people is combined. There is now a mobile phone app so that records can be submitted while still out in the field. You don't have to be into listing birds to contribute records to BirdTrack, though some of the most useful submissions are in the form

of complete species lists for defined sites and periods of time.*
And it's likely that a high proportion of records are submitted
by individuals motivated, at least in part, by adding to one or
other of their lists.

Jennifer Owen's remarkable *Wildlife of a Garden* describes a
thirty-year study of her small Leicester garden during which no
fewer than 2,600 species were identified.† The bird total is modest
at just 54 species but she includes over 300 moths, 80 spiders,
90 hoverflies and 440 beetles in the grand total. The whole
endeavour is centred on seeing or trapping species so that they
can be identified and recorded. The book is full of lists but it is
also so much more than that. It contains insights and analyses
of relevance to anyone with an interest in wildlife and how we
have impacted upon it over recent decades. Despite her impressive species total she falls well short of the leaders of a growing
movement of 'pan-species' listers in Britain. Their simple aim is
to identify and record as many species as possible from any

---

* See the BTO website (search for 'BirdTrack') for more information. The reason
complete species lists are so useful is that they allow reliable comparisons to be made
between the relative abundance of different species or, for individual species, between
different time periods. For example, if a species features on roughly 2% of complete
lists over a period of years but this subsequently falls to only 0.5%, a substantial
decline in abundance is suggested. Selective records, rather than complete lists, are
less reliable because biases can be introduced depending on the fortunes of the species
in question. As a bird declines people may become more inclined to note and record
any individuals they see. The opposite is true for common and widespread species,
which are more likely to be taken for granted and therefore under-reported. Many
taxonomic groups, in addition to birds, have their own recording schemes, and even
their own mobile apps; almost all records of species can contribute to wider understanding if compiled into lists and sent to the right place.
† Owen, J. (2010) *Wildlife of a Garden: A Thirty-Year Study*. Royal Horticultural
Society, Peterborough.

taxonomic group. At the time of writing, to get to the top of the pile you would need to have seen almost 12,000 species.

While pan-species listing might appear to be at the extreme end of listing behaviour, eclipsing even the most rabid of twitchers, it has two significant points in its favour. First, the more taxonomic groups you are interested in the less need there is to travel large distances in order to make new discoveries. Adding to your list relies more on building up expertise and identification skills (and using them locally) than on roaming the country from top to bottom. After all, Jennifer Owen managed over 2,600 species in a small suburban garden. The second point relates to the widely mourned loss of the competent all-round field naturalist in Britain and the resulting lack of individuals capable of surveying and recording the full range of our wildlife, especially some of the more obscure and unloved groups. Could pan-species listing help to encourage a new generation of skilled, all-round observers able to fill that void?*

It may sound feeble, but the prospect of adding species to my local patch list really does help get me out of the house and into the countryside. The chance of seeing something new on any given day is small. The addition of new birds has reduced to a trickle, though the slower the trickle the more enjoyable each new addition becomes. The chances of finding a bird I have yet to see in Britain are, admittedly, remote, though the possibility crosses my mind occasionally as I walk out through the gate. But despite decades of almost daily visits to the countryside there

---

* Google 'pan-species listing' for a surprising number of links relating to this subject, and for the 'official' website hosted by the Biological Records Centre.

are still high-profile, enigmatic vertebrates that I have yet to encounter, including species that are reasonably common and widespread. Some, like the various bats, are nocturnal and difficult to identify without specialist expertise. Others are easy to identify and can be readily seen during daylight. It's just a case of being in the right place at the right time and being observant enough to notice. Two on my radar are seen regularly in the Fens, and while I don't know for sure they are present on the local patch, I wouldn't be at all surprised. The drains and ditches with their rank vegetation certainly seem suitable. I hope it's only a matter of time before Harvest Mouse and Water Shrew are finally added to my mammal list – though, until that happens, their absence will help ensure that I keep on looking.

Postscript

When we later moved to Devon I did, finally, manage to catch up with the Harvest Mouse, no more than a few metres from the front door of our new house. After several decades of waiting, it was an experience fully as delightful as I had anticipated (see *A change of scene*). The Water Shrew has been less cooperative. The thought of chancing upon one still has me peering hopefully into streams and rivers when out and about in the local countryside, so far without success.

A LOVE OF BIRDS?

As a child I hated it when friends or family referred to me as a 'bird-lover'. The term 'birdwatcher' was fine, and later, when it caught on, 'birder' was even better. But 'bird-lover' was problematic even if, at the time, I didn't understand why. Several decades on, I think I can finally offer an explanation.

I was reminded of this recently when flicking through one of the RSPB's conservation science publications. There was a short profile of Professor Rhys Green in which he described how his relatives kept trying to give him animals to look after when he was young, based on his interest in wildlife. He was less than impressed: 'I don't want to have a relationship with an animal, I want to understand how it works as another being.' I feel the same way. I enjoy watching wildlife and learning about how animals use their environment. And I'm concerned about the status of populations; I want reassurance that we'll be able to carry on watching and learning about them in future. But I don't want to have a relationship with individual birds – and that, to me, is what is implied by the term 'bird-lover'.

Perhaps a brief example will help. I have often watched predators try to catch and kill prey. Although only a small proportion of attacks are successful, they provide moments of high drama, when life hangs precariously in the balance. I've been lucky enough to watch Merlins chasing after Skylarks in the Fens in winter, when the 'moment' of drama extends to several minutes. The Skylark endeavours to escape by flying up in tight circles, jinking in response to each attack to avoid capture. The Merlin's approach is one of persistence, with attacks repeated many times as the two birds spiral upwards. The aim is to wear down the potential prey until it becomes so weak that it can be taken. Sometimes a Skylark will sing as it is chased. That requires extra energy, but if it serves to demonstrate just how fit and strong the bird is, it may cause the attacker to think twice about wasting energy in a prolonged pursuit. Deer employ a similar tactic when they make those exaggerated vertical jumps on all four legs when threatened by a predator.

When watching predators at work I feel no real compassion for either the predator (which may be desperate to eat) or the prey (which I'm sure is desperate to avoid being eaten). In the case of the Merlin and the Skylark, if anything I slightly favour the aggressor, not through any blood-lust but because witnessing a bird of prey successfully catching something is such a rare and privileged event. These moments offer thrilling insights into how two species interact, and how both have evolved behaviours, honed down the millennia, to help them survive. They help us to better understand how wildlife works. I love the spectacle, but not the individual players.

Not everyone feels this way, and it's striking just how different human reactions can be to the death of a bird. For people who put out food for garden birds, a visit from the local Sparrowhawk (or worse, the local cat) might be genuinely upsetting. And the distress may be accentuated if familiar individuals, recognisable from their distinctive plumage or behaviour, are predated. I can sympathise to some extent, though these birds really are part-way to becoming pets if their loss is mourned at the level of the individual. At the opposite end of the spectrum are those who are so comfortable with predation they are happy to take on the role themselves, either for sport or for the pot (or a happy combination of the two).* I have spoken to wildfowlers who have a genuine fondness for the species they hunt. On one occasion a male Teal, shot just a few minutes previously, was lifted from the game bag to help make the point. I have admired the delicate, intricately inscribed, plumage of Teal through a telescope many times. Here was someone happy to do exactly the same thing with a bird he had just killed. For the reasons touched on earlier I see no great inconsistency in this. Skylarks brighten up the summers around here with their prolonged outpourings of song. And in winter their throaty chirrups as they rise up from the otherwise barren fields add texture and vitality to the landscape. They are one of my favourite birds. Yet it is a real thrill to watch one disappear into the local food chain.

---

* As an aside, it's interesting that some people formerly comfortable with shooting or hunting animals for sport turn away from it in later life and come to derive greater pleasure from watching wildlife than from killing it. It is rare indeed that this transformation takes place in the opposite direction. Is this the result of the increasing wisdom that comes with age, or is it simply that the instinctive pleasure humans take in pursuing and killing animals is stronger in young people and tends to fade later in life? I have occasionally resorted to lethal control of wildlife to protect the garden vegetable plot or to deal with infestations of rats, but I find it more and more difficult to pull the trigger as I get older.

UNWELCOME WILDLIFE

I have just returned from our annual family holiday with my parents, Brian and Margaret, and my sister Jacks and her family. This year we rented a cottage near Polzeath in north Cornwall, and spent a relaxing week walking the coastal cliffs, rock-pooling and 'surfing' on the local beach. There wasn't much time for serious wildlife watching, though throughout the week I was struck by how often wildlife kept intervening in unwelcome ways, at least from the perspective of most members of my family. It started soon after we arrived. The noticeboard in the hall included a stark message alerting us to the fact that the village was 'plagued with Badgers', together with dire warnings about the consequences of leaving rubbish bags out overnight. Discussions followed as to how we were going to deal with our refuse and deliver it safely to the collectors, without the Badgers getting to it first.

I already had suspicions that wildlife could interfere with the surfing part of the holiday, based on expressions of concern during the long drive from home. I thought I dealt well enough with worries about sharks, pointing out that in nearly fifty years I'd never even seen one when swimming in the sea, never mind been threatened by one. I fared rather less well in relation to jellyfish.

Yes, they can sting (some of them); yes, I suppose I had often seen them when swimming in the sea; yes, warmer conditions in recent years had resulted in greatly increased numbers; yes, certain species could kill humans (though this was very rare); and no, I thought it unlikely that I'd be willing to urinate on anyone unfortunate enough to be stung, not on a public beach with hundreds of people watching. I did, though, point out that we all had wetsuits and I didn't think they could sting through those.

As luck would have it, we saw very few jellyfish during the week. Instead, surfing concerns centred around a small vertebrate that enjoys hiding in the sand within the surf zone, the much-feared Lesser Weever Fish. Having been warned by locals that they were in the area, members of our party googled the offending creature, quickly learning that the dorsal fin is made up of many razor-sharp spines, each one with sufficient poison to inflict excruciating pain on anything that interferes with it. This heavy weaponry is designed to prevent predation by larger fish but, as one of the RNLI lifeguards told us, it is not selective. On a single day the previous week he had dealt with at least ten cases where unsuspecting human feet had been injected with poison. A bucket of hot water, rather than a stream of hot urine, was his suggested remedy. In the end we invested in spine-proof rubber water shoes to go with our wetsuits and the children had a great time once they had finally plucked up enough courage to enter the water.

Wildlife regularly causes us minor inconveniences and irritations of this sort. Gulls steal our chips in resorts where they have overcome their fear of humans. They also cause problems if they are nesting on roof tops in urban areas. Their raucous calls from first light are not appreciated by light sleepers. Worse still, the adults will sometimes defend their young vigorously, dive-bombing people who stray too close. Then there are wasps to fend off in the summer, and mosquitoes, midges and horse flies seeking to feast on our blood. There are plants that can sting us and berries that make us ill (or worse) if consumed carelessly. Rabbits, deer and slugs can all wreak havoc with lovingly nurtured vegetable plots and flowerbeds.

I was once phoned at work by an ardent football supporter whose television had stopped working in the middle of the World Cup finals. His *leylandii* hedge had grown so high it had started to interfere with the signal reaching the satellite dish on the side of his house. He was about to start cutting back the trees to rectify the problem when he noticed a Collared Dove nest with small chicks. What could he do (I was asked), bearing in mind that England had a vital game in a few days and he was very keen to watch it? While I sympathised, my advice was not what he wanted to hear. He couldn't continue with the hedge cutting because that would have destroyed the nest and the young birds it contained. While farmers can legally kill Collared Doves in their hundreds to protect crops and food stores, there is nothing in the legislation to cater for frustrated football fans. He would have to wait until the young doves had left the nest. Until then he would need to find somewhere else to watch the football.

Less often, wildlife causes problems that go beyond minor irritation. Woodpigeons reduce crop yields by descending en masse to feed. Foxes break into poultry farms and kill dozens of birds at a time, and Cormorants remove valuable stocked fish from ponds and lakes. My wife Hazel used to work as a 'wildlife advisor' (for Natural England), dispensing advice, and sometimes licences, to people adversely affected by protected species. Badgers cause more than their fair share of problems by virtue of their earth-moving capabilities. They damage lawns, undermine buildings, destabilise flood-defence banks and even dig up graveyards. One problem she dealt with involved children playing in a garden next to a churchyard. Parental intervention revealed that an object they were tossing back and forth to each other was a human skull, dug out by Badgers on the boundary between the two properties.

The solutions to problems caused by wildlife vary. Woodpigeons and Foxes can legally be killed to prevent losses. Cormorants can also be shot, though a licence is required first. Problems caused by Badgers are usually dealt with by excluding them from their sett, again under licence. One-way gates are installed so they can leave but are unable to return, in the hope that they will find somewhere less problematic to set up home.

At the top of the scale of wildlife impacts are the rare occasions when encounters with humans result in loss of life. Great White Sharks, Lions, Tigers, Grizzly Bears, crocodiles, venomous snakes and spiders all take their toll in different parts of the world. Even here in Britain people are occasionally killed by wildlife. Wasp stings, Adder bites and the misidentification of plants or fungi when collecting for the pot have all resulted in untimely deaths. Deer are probably our biggest killers, thanks to the accidents caused when they run out unexpectedly onto busy roads. Pheasants too cause accidents when dopey, captive-reared birds spill onto our highways in their dozens in the autumn.

While all these impacts are, of course, unwelcome, I can't help but find the inconveniences imposed by our wildlife strangely (some might say perversely) reassuring. On holiday in Polzeath, I was delighted that Badgers were 'plaguing' the village. We found their dung pits on the footpath nearby and even snuffle holes in the lawn where they had been searching for food. We didn't see the animals themselves, but the possibility that we might bump into one added to late-evening excursions into the garden. Having to find somewhere inside to store our refuse until bin day was surely a small price to pay.

If my family could just about understand that line of reasoning, they were not convinced that the Lesser Weever Fish added anything positive to the week. After all, this creature had sparked genuine alarm and meant that we'd had to fork out for extra footwear. And yet, despite the problems, these animals provide welcome reassurance that humans are not in complete control. Despite our huge impacts on the environment and apparent mastery of nature, there are still animals out there that cause us problems. They exist even though we (some of us, at least) wish they didn't. Part of the enjoyment I derive from an interest in wildlife is the sense of release it provides in a high-pressure world dominated by humans. We didn't see any weever fish, just as we didn't see any Badgers. But we knew they were there, and they added something 'wild' to the experience of splashing around in the surf, even as we shared the waves with hundreds of other people.

To move back up the scale of impacts, the presence of animals that are capable of inflicting serious harm dramatically changes the way I feel about an area and its wildlife, in a way that is also surprisingly positive. The experience of walking in parts of Canada and the United States, where both Black and Grizzly Bears are still present, is truly thrilling. The chance of being attacked is minuscule (provided common sense is followed) but it is there nevertheless and, for me, that fundamentally alters the experience. I feel a heightened sense of awareness to the sights and sounds of the countryside, and with that comes a connection to the natural world that is somehow more deep-rooted, more meaningful and more inspiring.

On holiday a few years ago Hazel and I were struggling to find our way back to the car, parked somewhere on a remote forest track in Grand Teton National Park in Wyoming. The light was fading, it was getting cold and we were genuinely concerned that we would not make it back before nightfall. The only walkable route was a thin, winding strip of land with impenetrable forest on one side and marshy, unstable, bog on the other. Prints in the snow showed that other animals had also used this route, including a bear. About an hour earlier we had startled a Black Bear within the forest, but we knew that this area also supported the more dangerous Grizzly Bear. Being forced to follow a bear trail in fading light, miles from the nearest human habitation, was truly memorable. Although it felt genuinely frightening at the time, we were in no real danger and I reflect on it now as an entirely positive experience. We have long since lost our top predators in Britain, and with them we have lost a significant part of our connection with the wild.

I once felt much the same about severe weather as I do now about disruptive or predatory wildlife. Gales, heavy snow and thunderstorms were always rather comforting and reassuring, despite the disruption they caused. In fact, largely *because* of the disruption they caused. Such events were beyond our control and showed that nature could still operate on its own terms, much like the Lesser Weever Fish lying beneath the sand or the Grizzly Bears lurking around the next corner. I'm using the past tense because the impact of climate change has dulled my enjoyment of extreme weather. While it's not possible to attribute any single extreme event to climate change, the models all predict that they will become more frequent. The same extreme weather that, in my childhood, symbolised wild nature, now serves only to highlight the all-pervasive and largely negative influence of humanity.

THE SOUND OF SILENCE

We all enjoy a bit of peace and quiet; a break from the usual barrage of artificial sounds associated with modern living. I certainly appreciate places where natural sounds are dominant. Ironically, as I've got older and my hearing has started to deteriorate, I find it even more desirable, though less and less easy, to find quiet places. That might appear counterintuitive but there is some logic to it. As my hearing has worsened, I've found it increasingly difficult to pick out singing or calling birds, particularly those with high-pitched voices. And it has become *especially* difficult to hear birds in an environment with lots of background noise.

It's much the same when talking to people. Quiet meeting rooms are fine but trying to hold a conversation in the lunch break when everyone is talking is not so easy. On the Tube in London, hearing what people say has become so difficult that I'm reminded of the Michael McIntyre sketch in which he points out that you can only reasonably ask someone to repeat themselves three times. After that you are obliged, by an unwritten but universally agreed rule, to guess what was said and to try

This chapter is based on an article first published in the January 2019 issue of *British Birds* (112: 2–3).

to respond meaningfully: 'I don't disagree' or 'I know what you mean' are helpful catch-all phrases.

I've not been able to hear calling Goldcrests, or shrews or bats, for decades; so long, in fact, that I've started to question whether I ever could hear them. But I'm sure I could as a child. I have memories of diving into vegetation to find squabbling shrews, something that would be unthinkable now as I pass by, oblivious to their presence. Even crickets and grasshoppers are now merely visible, rather than audible, features of the country-side. A sound that is (so I'm told) highly evocative of summer in much of Britain has been completely lost to me. People sometimes struggle to believe my hearing is so poor that I can't hear them, to the extent that every new stridulating individual is gleefully pointed out: 'Can you hear that?' 'Surely you can hear *that* one?' 'What about this one – it's hurting my ear drums?' I'm tempted to lie just to end the pantomime.

I don't really miss listening to grasshoppers, or bats or shrews, because I haven't been able to hear them for such a long time. Any pleasure they once brought has been lost from memory. But I do miss quiet places. And I find it rather depressing that it has become almost impossible to find places free from artificial noise across large parts of the country.

Last autumn I did stumble upon a place free from anthropo-genic noise. I was walking along the western bank of the huge Ouse Washes nature reserve, south of the village of Welney in Norfolk. I'd walked from the road but was now at least three kilometres away from it, and with a helpful wind direction the hum of traffic had long since faded out. A railway line crosses the washes a few kilometres further on but it was Sunday morning and few trains were running. There were no military jets from the nearby Breckland airfields (Sunday again) and no gas guns within earshot, presumably because, in early September, we were 'between crops'. Anything that might otherwise have been set upon by ravenous Woodpigeons had either already been harvested or was yet to be planted. There were no other roads nearby, and two distant farmsteads were the only buildings visible.

It wasn't completely silent, but the faint noises I could detect were all natural: a light breeze blowing through the leaves of bankside willows, the soft babble of Rooks and Jackdaws on stubbles a few fields away, and small fish gently rippling the surface of the river. It felt more than a little surreal. Then, just as I was contemplating how unusual this was, a distant, revving motorbike broke the spell. I waited for it to pass but then saw a tractor heading slowly up the farm track towards me and that was that. It was back to normality.

As well as intruding on our enjoyment of the countryside, excessive background noise has consequences for wildlife. Studies have found that high levels of traffic noise can reduce the diversity of birds in adjacent habitats, and reduce the density of breeding birds in some species. Young House Sparrows are fed less frequently at noisy nest sites because the adults are less able to hear their begging calls. A study on Lundy Island off the north Devon coast found that nestlings near a noisy generator grew more slowly than expected, and fewer survived to join the local population.* Other studies have shown that nestlings beg

---

* Schroeder, J., Nakagawa, S., Cleasby, I. R. and Burke, T. (2012) Passerine birds breeding under chronic noise experience reduced fitness. *PLoS One* 7: e39200.

more loudly and persistently at noisy sites in order to be heard, though this has the downside of making them more obvious to predators.

Great Tits in busy urban areas now sing songs that are measurably different from those heard in quieter rural locations. The urban birds use a higher pitch that's easier for other birds to hear above the din of the traffic. Similar adjustments, incidentally, have been made by birds in response to increasing levels of artificial light, prolonging the period during which they sing at night. These effects are subtle and localised, though less so with every passing year, but they represent yet another human impact tilting the balance in favour of species that are flexible and adaptable. Those with more discerning requirements or a preference for more natural conditions lose out, once again.

If you have doubts about how difficult it is to find quiet places in our modern countryside, at least during daylight hours, bear it in mind next time you venture outdoors. It may be more difficult than you think to experience silence, even if you live in a remote rural area. If you are unable to find peace and quiet easily, then the obvious question is: How much does that bother you? From the conversations I've had, the answer for many people might be 'not much at all'. If so, perhaps this is just another example of 'shifting baseline syndrome'. This expression describes how our expectations are based mainly on our own experiences, rather than on what the evidence suggests might be obtainable, or what existed in the past. The term is sometimes used by conservationists when describing how expectations for wildlife populations (and habitats) are constantly reset – like a ratchet slowly and invisibly tightening its grip on the landscape. With a species that has been in long-term decline, we no longer aspire to return the population to its original level. The aspirational baseline is more likely to be reset to a level with which we are familiar from our own memories. I have long forgotten the noises made by shrews, bats and grasshoppers, and I no longer mourn the loss of these sounds from my life. For many of us, I think that now applies to peace and quiet in the countryside. We don't much miss it because we've forgotten what it sounds like.

HEALTH-ENHANCING
HOUSE MARTINS

We hear more and more about how nature is good for us, something I think I've always been intuitively aware of. Partly it's just common sense. Any hobby makes us feel better about life if it's enjoyable and gets the body and brain working a bit more. Walking, playing football, gardening, photography, doing the crossword and watching wildlife are all good for you if that's your thing. And yet the claims made on behalf of nature go much further. Having some green space (and its attendant wildlife) in our communities is good for all of us. The scientific research is unequivocal. To take one of a growing number of examples, studies show that if you can see trees or gardens from your hospital bed, rather than bland concrete walls, you are likely to recover from illness more quickly and require less pain-relieving medication. Looking out over trees and being able to 'connect with nature' at a basic level has a sufficiently strong effect on the human brain to measurably improve health.

I had cause to reflect on this during a recent visit to hospital. I was at Addenbrooke's in Cambridge one day in early September, and although it was for nothing more onerous than a routine scan, I was not in the brightest of moods. The thought of sliding into the bowels of one of those full-body MRI scanners was not an appealing one. The stark concrete buildings did nothing to ease the sense of foreboding. Not far from the main entrance, though, I noticed something that instantly improved my state of mind. It reminded me of all the studies about the health benefits of wildlife and, at the same time, made them seem believable. High up, under the eaves of the fourth floor of the main building, was a large House Martin colony, buzzing with frenetic end-of-season activity. There were dozens of the dome-shaped mud nests, all crammed together along a short stretch of overhang. The birds were swarming back and forth, brightening an otherwise uninspiring backdrop of glass, concrete and grey sky, despite their monochrome plumage. Even with my poor hearing, I could make out their soft contact calls, rippling gently but persistently above the drone of hospital traffic.

The House Martin is one of just a handful of birds able to pull off the trick of being almost entirely dependent on humanity while remaining largely indifferent to humans. Although almost the entire British population now nests on our houses, bridges and utility buildings, you'd be hard pushed to elicit any kind of direct response from a House Martin, short of poking your face directly into its nest. It's a trait that puts this bird high up on my list of favourites. Amidst the traffic and the concrete, here is one of the most independent and therefore 'wildest' birds you can expect to see – a cut above the scrounging House Sparrows, Starlings and Feral Pigeons, vying unashamedly for our scraps and hand-outs.

There is another black-and-white bird that makes use of our buildings and brightens our urban areas, while remaining largely independent of people. It flocks together in hundreds, even thousands, to roost at the end of each day in winter. Unlike the House Martin, it is not beyond filching a few crumbs in public places, but most of its food is invertebrates, hard-won, without human assistance. Pied Wagtails gravitate towards places with expanses of concrete and tarmac both for foraging and for roosting, including shopping centres, car parks, service stations and hospitals. It's almost as if they are selecting the sites that are most in need of cheering up.

Having watched the House Martin colony for half an hour, I headed inside for my appointment, realising that I was now in a far better frame of mind. I imagined just how much difference these birds might have made, had I required a longer stay here. Yet, of the hundreds of people passing by during the time I was looking up at the birds, not one so much as glanced in their direction. I've noticed much the same thing when watching gatherings of Pied Wagtails in urban areas. I wondered if any of the hospital patients ever watched the House Martins at the colony from their window and derived any pleasure from them – and I guessed that few would give them a second look. It was a reminder that 'nature' and 'conservation' means different things to different people. Almost everyone appreciates a bit of green space and a few trees, but most people don't focus on (or even care much about) the roll call of species that such areas support. Perhaps only keen birdwatchers have much to gain from something as individual as a House Martin colony.

ADOPT A SPECIES

This is not going to be one of those pleas to help raise money for conservation. It is, instead, a suggestion, based on something that happened to me by accident back in the mid-1990s, something that has made a huge difference to the way I think about birds and other animals.

For eight years, from 1995, I worked for English Nature (now Natural England) on the Red Kite reintroduction project. That time was spent focusing, primarily, on just one species. Much of the job was taken up with monitoring the released birds: trying to find out as much as possible about their behaviour and ecology, and how they fitted into a landscape from which they had been absent for so long. I learnt a lot and I wrote two books about the Red Kite which summarise what is known about the bird and what has been achieved by the reintroduction project.* I thoroughly enjoyed getting to know this bird intimately, but it surprised me just how helpful this knowledge was when I was watching other species. Having got to know one bird well, I found I had a useful reference point against which the traits of

---

* Carter, I. (2007) *The Red Kite*, 2nd edition. Arlequin Press, Shrewsbury. Carter, I. and Powell, D. (2019) *The Red Kite's Year*. Pelagic Publishing, Exeter.

other species could be compared, contrasted and made more memorable.

Radio-tracking of Red Kites showed that they tend to forage within about three or four kilometres of their nest. Males tend to travel furthest from the nest, while females usually remain within a kilometre or two. I was astonished when I first read that Turtle Doves can forage anything up to ten kilometres from their nest sites – twice the maximum distance that I had ever recorded for a Red Kite. Even small finches, including the humble Linnet, fly several kilometres to find suitable seeding plants in the breeding season – a bird no more than 2 per cent of the weight of a Red Kite, travelling a similar distance in order to gather food for its young. The advantage that the Turtle Dove and Linnet have is their ability to regurgitate food for their nestlings. In contrast, the Red Kite must carry individual food items back to the nest site, which is onerous and limits the area over which it can usefully forage.

The Buzzard provides a contrast in the other direction. This bird is highly territorial. Breeding pairs find all their food within well-defended home ranges, often considerably smaller than one square kilometre. That's a tiny fraction of the area used by the Red Kite, which is under no such territorial constraints. In areas with a high density of Buzzards, a single male Red Kite might wander through the territories of twenty or thirty pairs of Buzzards when searching for food during the breeding season. These two birds are roughly the same size and are found in the same areas. They build similar nests in similar places and they eat many of the same things. We may regard them as similar birds. And yet they use the landscape in radically different ways.

Even with my poor memory, the key timings of the Red Kite's breeding season are firmly lodged in my mind, having been reinforced by long days in the field trying to locate pairs and follow their progress through the season. Pairs start to spend more time near the breeding site in late winter, begin nest building in March, lay eggs in the first half of April and have young in the nest from about mid-May until mid-July. Young are seen around the nest area for a further month or so but, by late August, most will have melted away into the surrounding countryside. I find this framework invaluable when thinking about other species with very different breeding seasons. The Grey Heron, for example, breeds early in the year. The young are already flapping vigorously in the nest by the time Red Kites get around to laying their first egg. In contrast, late-arriving migrants such as Montagu's Harriers and Honey-buzzards are only just making landfall in southern England when the kites are busy feeding their newly hatched chicks. Most Swifts arrive in Britain when Red Kites are part-way through the incubation period. And most will be well on their way back to Africa by the time the year's new intake of kites are fully grown and independent of their parents.

The benefits of knowing a species intimately extend beyond behavioural aspects. Having a good feel for the size of Red Kite populations provides another useful reference. There are close to one million pairs of Buzzards in Europe according to the latest estimates. In isolation it's tricky to think about what that means. Is it a lot? Perhaps, though presumably a lot less than it should be given the impacts of persecution and habitat loss. The picture becomes clearer if you consider that the Buzzard is about forty times more abundant in Europe than the Red Kite (at around

26,000 pairs). In fact, in Britain alone, we have roughly three pairs of Buzzards for every one pair of the world's Red Kites. Applying the same logic to a few other species, we find that Britain has thirty-five pairs of Guillemot, five pairs of Mallard, fourteen pairs of Fulmar and 0.5 pairs of Ring-necked Parakeet for each of the world's Red Kite pairs. Rather more worryingly, for every pair of Red Kites on the planet, more than 1,500 non-native Pheasants are released into our lowland countryside every year.

All this information can, of course, be appreciated in isolation. But I find the in-built Red Kite reference points help me no end when considering the behaviour and status of other birds; and it means that I'm far more likely to retain the facts in my mind. I'm not suggesting everyone will want to devote eight years of their life to a single species, though it's not a bad way to spend the time. But I would certainly recommend getting to know a favoured local species as intimately as possible. Try to become something of an expert on that chosen animal, and your appreciation and understanding of wildlife more generally will be greatly enhanced.

WANTED: DEAD OR ALIVE

I couldn't agree more with Conor Jameson when he describes how he has 'mixed feelings' when he finds a dead animal.* I share the same feelings and, like Conor, have also been accused of taking a macabre interest in the flattened corpses that litter our modern roads.

While the loss of life is regrettable, dead animals provide useful information about the wildlife of an area, some of which is otherwise difficult to come by. For a start, roadkill offers a rapid and effective way of surveying some species. A squashed Hedgehog shows that this declining species is still hanging on in the area. I often notice them on roads through the Fens in what looks like rather unpromising, arable-dominated, habitat. But I see them most often on roads in and around villages, which tells us something useful about their habitat preferences. The diversity provided by village gardens with their lawns, flowerbeds, rockeries and bushes is clearly a more welcoming prospect than the surrounding arable prairies. The Badger is another nocturnal species whose regular death on fenland roads shows, paradoxically, that it is alive and well in the area.

---

* Jameson, C. M. (2014) *Shrewdunnit: The Nature Files*. Pelagic Publishing, Exeter.

One advantage of road-kills is that there is a body to examine, and that can sometimes produce information that is impossible to glean from a brief sighting of a live animal. In fact, a body is almost essential to confirm the identity of certain animals that are otherwise very tricky to get to grips with. I have yet to find a pure-bred Polecat on my travels in eastern England, but close inspection of several corpses has shown that hybrid Polecat–Ferrets are present. A dead Wildcat on a road through dense forest in Hungary allowed us a full appreciation of the exquisite markings of this animal, including the wonderful, thick, richly banded tail. It meant we could be completely confident that it was the real thing rather than a semi-domestic imposter – something not so easy with a live animal glimpsed through the trees or darting across a road. To reinforce the point, we did later see a live one, and although we saw it well and noted all the key characteristics, its proximity to a village left a small but nagging element of doubt.

On a recent trip to Washington state and British Columbia the roadkill mammal list included Raccoon, Virginia Opossum, Porcupine and any number of skunks. The latter, like small, asymmetrical, black-and-white rugs glued to the tarmac, could be identified even at close to 100 kilometres per hour from the distinctive smell that somehow permeated the interior of the car. We never did see a live one. Back in Britain I can say the same about the Brown Long-eared Bat, an animal I've only ever seen as a corpse, found in the back garden. In the hand it looked faintly ridiculous with its oversized ears protruding from an improbably tiny body.

As I've got older, I've overcome my embarrassment at stopping the car to inspect dead animals, even if there are passengers on board. I insist on stopping for Barn Owls, if possible, as this species is well monitored in the Fens, where the majority breed in boxes. A dead bird has a high chance of carrying a ring. Recoveries of ringed individuals are heavily biased towards road casualties, but even so they provide valuable information on survival rates and dispersal patterns.

When I was involved in the Red Kite project I had a good chance of locating any dead birds through the radio-tags they carried. This brought the same mixed feelings described above, only heightened. Even the loss of a single bird in the early stages of a reintroduction increases the chances that the project will fail. Then there is the poignancy of handling the lifeless body of a bird that had been collected as a nestling in Spain, fed daily in pens for several weeks and then, finally, released to fly free in the wild. All that, only to end up lying dead in an English field before having the chance to pair up and contribute something to the fledgling population. Still, the whole point of fitting radio-tags to released birds is to gather information, including information about why birds die. So, amidst feelings of frustration (amplified in the case of birds killed illegally), there was satisfaction that the monitoring technology had worked. As a result, another fragment of information would be added to our knowledge of the threats faced by Red Kites in our modern landscapes.

It's good to see that Conor Jameson and I are far from alone in taking an interest in road casualties. Project Splatter is the name given to an unusual citizen science project led by scientists at Cardiff University.* It seeks to quantify and map wildlife

---

* Project Splatter: https://projectsplatter.co.uk.

roadkill across the UK. Anyone can report observations of dead birds, mammals, reptiles and amphibians, and more than 50,000 records have already been submitted. The project aims to raise awareness of this issue, identify hotspots where lots of animals are killed and, ultimately, help try to reduce the extent of the problem. People have come up with all manner of ways to pass the time on long, tedious car journeys. Here is another excellent option.

THE STATE OF NATURE

What is the current state of our wildlife and the habitats on which it depends, in Britain and across the rest of the world? It's clear that we have lost more and more of our wild places over recent centuries. And the evidence shows that declines have continued to the present day, if anything picking up pace. But the last few decades have also seen a huge growth in conservation organisations, and in measures designed to help limit the losses and to protect the best remaining areas of habitat. So how successful have we been in protecting wildlife and wild places? This is a fundamental question for anyone interested in the natural world, but it is surprisingly difficult to answer. To borrow a thought from Simon Barnes, our response is likely to be based less on knowledge and sound reasoning than on temperament or even mood.*

When trying to understand an issue I find it useful to think in terms of extremes. In this case, one extreme would be the landscape and wildlife of Britain before humans started to modify it. Or, if you prefer, try to imagine what we would have now in the absence of any past human interventions. There has

---

* Barnes, S. (2014) The long-term view. *British Wildlife* 26: 2–9.

been much debate about the extent to which Britain would once have been blanketed with forest. Would the Red Squirrel really have been able to make it from Cornwall to Caithness without descending to ground level? Despite knowledge gaps, the broad picture is clear enough. Wilderness, with a high proportion of forest, once covered the landscape, and the full suite of native species, including major predators, roamed the land.

At the other extreme is the 'nightmare scenario' we could end up with, perhaps a few hundred years from now (or perhaps sooner), where every scrap of land is required to support humanity and there is nothing left for wildlife. All land has either been built on or enclosed. All our food is produced under cover in sterile growing areas where the climate is artificially controlled and wildlife excluded. Wild animals are known only from books, websites and a few token representatives in the handful of remaining zoos. We live in the Holocene epoch (meaning 'entirely recent'), although many people already refer to the Anthropocene, a name that reflects the all-pervasive influence of our own species on the planet. The renowned American biologist and theorist E. O. Wilson has gone further, suggesting this may give way to what he calls the Eremocene, or 'age of loneliness'.*

We are a long way away from either of the two extreme scenarios. It's a subjective judgement, but you could make a case that we are somewhere close to halfway between them. On the one hand, in Britain at least, almost all our truly natural habitats have been lost. We are left with tiny fragments of near-natural

---

* Wilson, E. O. (2014) *The Meaning of Human Existence*. Liveright Publishing Corporation, New York.

habitat and larger 'semi-natural' areas, all greatly modified by human activity. The influence of people, and our crops, livestock and pollutants, is everywhere. Some of our most enigmatic wild animals, including top predators such as Lynx, Wolves and Brown Bears, and large herbivores including the Bison, Moose and Aurochs have been consigned to history. On the other hand, we are a long way from having concreted over the entire country. Wildlife has been heavily influenced by people but it remains as a highly visible presence all around us, with considerable diversity remaining. Most of the native birds that recolonised Britain after the last major glaciation, roughly 10,000 years ago, are still with us. If you own a garden you can glance out of the window and see wild birds going about their business as they have done for thousands of generations.

Which brings us back to the point about temperament. Your view of the current 'state of nature' probably says something about whether you are an optimist or a pessimist. Is the glass half full or half empty? Do you focus on the huge gap between what we have now and the nightmare scenario where there is virtually nothing natural left, and count your blessings that we have something worth fighting for? Or do you contrast what we have now with the far richer and wilder countryside of the past, and sink into despair? To put it another way, do you think mostly about all the amazing wildlife we have lost, or about all the amazing wildlife we have yet to lose?

I flip regularly between despair and positivity, depending on mood. My state of mind can be dramatically influenced by a walk from the house into the local countryside. There are days when wildlife seems to be everywhere, thriving despite the changes we have made, and in some cases because of them. The fields are full of Brown Hares, there is fresh digging at the Badger sett, and I notice Fox prints and Otter spraint along the main fen drain. A cloud of gulls is following a tractor and the next field has flocks of Skylarks, Starlings, Lapwing and Golden Plover all scraping a living from the land. There appears to be enough wildlife to support predators at the top of the food chain. I see a stunning male Hen Harrier crisscrossing the fields as well as a distant Peregrine and two different Barn Owls hugging the grassy field margins. On another day it's a struggle to see more than a handful of animals on the same walk and pessimism takes over. The arable fields are devoid of life – eliminated, so it seems, by intensive agriculture and its lack of tolerance for anything that interferes with the growing crops.

My mood can also be flipped from one state to another by wildlife magazines, websites or natural history programmes on TV. We are constantly bombarded by two highly contrasting visions of the natural world, not so far removed from the extreme scenarios I've described. On the one hand there are inspiring conservation success stories – species that have been brought back from the brink and are now thriving, and nature reserves teeming with wildlife just waiting for us to visit. We are told that we live in an amazing country with abundant and diverse wildlife all around us. Then there are stories about drastic declines in many of our once common and familiar species and warnings that they may soon be gone for good. I'm reminded that over 95 per cent of our wildflower-rich meadows and 80 per cent of our heathland has been lost in the last 200 years; that just 2 per cent of Britain now comprises ancient woodland, and much of that is still unprotected and at risk from development. I can read an issue of *BBC Wildlife* and be left reeling. There are inspiring wild places to visit, but will they still be there by the time I get around to it?

In the end I lean towards optimism most of the time, through necessity rather than logic. What we have currently is sufficient. It has to be. If you are interested in wildlife, you are stuck with what is left and you have no choice but to make the best of it. Our brains are supremely good at adapting to situations as they are, rather than as they might have been. When I discuss conservation with others not fully converted to the cause they remind me that most of Britain is still 'countryside', the implication being that they are happy enough with the amount of green space and wildlife in this country. If we still had Brown Bears, Dalmatian Pelicans or Great Auks in Britain then a sighting of any one of them would enhance a day in the field. As it is, a glimpse of a Stoat, Water Vole or Turtle Dove is enough to lift the spirits – because that is all we can expect to find these days.

Our in-built homeostasis is a significant problem for conservation. It makes it difficult to generate the anger and the passion that would help stem further losses. It would be a great shame if, years from now, all it took to set the pulse racing was a Rabbit, a Rook or two, or a few Starlings, hanging on in one of the last pockets of undeveloped land. We are heading in that direction, though at a pace slow enough that most of us haven't really noticed.

URBAN WILDLIFE

We hear a lot these days about nature in urban areas. This reflects the fact that so many of us now live in urban environments, as well as demonstrating an increasing recognition of the benefits of regular contact with wildlife. There are plenty of urban dwellers who appreciate wildlife but are not willing (or perhaps are unable) to make regular trips out into the countryside. They rely on wildlife that can adapt and thrive in what might seem, initially, to be a rather unpromising environment.

Naturalists often highlight discrepancies between our low expectations of urban areas and the abundance and diversity of wildlife they actually support. In reality, it's not so surprising that towns and cities support wildlife. Structural complexity is an important component of wildlife habitat, and this is something urban areas have in abundance. The mix of buildings, open spaces, tree-lined roads and pockets of greenery in gardens and parks provides a wide range of opportunities. Natural sources of food are available wherever there is vegetation, lawns or parks. Then there is the artificial food provided by human residents – some willingly offered as hand-outs in gardens, and some supplied inadvertently through the scraps and leftovers found wherever people gather in numbers. Scavengers and opportunists can make a good living, as can the predators that feed on them.

On visits to central London I often see two species that exploit opposite ends of the vertical profile of this city, both of which are dependent, in different ways, on our leftovers. I'm always delighted to see 'tube mice' scampering around beneath the rails within even the busiest of Underground stations. They scour the inhospitable terrain for bits of discarded hamburger and not-quite-empty crisp packets. They must surely have the least healthy diet of any British mammal. It's difficult to imagine a more hostile environment when viewed from a human perspective: just a few centimetres of cramped space between the high-voltage tracks and the trains thundering along them. If they venture up onto the platform, they must contend with the added hazard of hundreds of trampling feet. Generations of these animals come and go without ever being exposed to natural light.

Once I emerge from the station into daylight my eyes are looking up not down, towards the other vertical extreme and the chance of seeing a very different animal. I scan the tops of the tallest buildings and the ledges beneath, hoping for a glimpse of the city's most celebrated avian resident. The Peregrine, like the House Mouse, depends on our scraps and leftovers, though in this case they have been processed into something more palatable by scavenging Feral Pigeons and Starlings.

Another animal I always look for is the Fox, though the best opportunities for seeing it are from the train heading into and out of London. The rail network provides linear scraps of habitat that are, paradoxically, both highly developed by humans and virtually free from direct human disturbance. For obvious reasons the lines are securely fenced off and people go there only occasionally to paint their incomprehensible graffiti onto the infrastructure or, more legitimately, when maintenance work is required. Even in the most densely populated parts of town these strips provide a refuge, and Foxes take full advantage, sometimes sunbathing just metres from the track, oblivious to the hordes of commuters streaming by. The structural complexity of built-up areas suits this species well, providing plenty of refuges from disturbance as well as a wide range of natural and artificial foods. Foxes will take earthworms from lawns and playing fields on damp evenings, perhaps move on to fallen fruit or berries beneath garden trees, before rounding off the night's foraging with a few scraps of unwanted takeaway on the empty early-morning pavements. Add to that the food deliberately put out by householders, and it's easy to see why Fox densities tend to be higher in urban areas than in the countryside.

In comparisons between urban areas and the more intensively managed parts of the countryside, our towns and cities may well come out on top in terms of their wildlife potential. As if to emphasise the point, the twenty-hectare field surrounding our house is currently a virtual desert of bare earth, having been ploughed several weeks ago and then sprayed (twice) to remove troublesome residual weeds. It's quite possible that there is not a single bird currently using it, and I flushed nothing when walking the dog around the perimeter at lunchtime. I would challenge anyone to find an equivalent-sized area of urban space similarly devoid of wildlife.

It's right that we celebrate urban wildlife. And it's certainly right that we try to make our cities as attractive as possible for wild animals and the people who enjoy watching them. But I sometimes wonder if we overdo the celebrations. You could read the more effusive accounts of urban wildlife and be forgiven for thinking that concreting over large parts of the country is not much of a problem, because wildlife will simply adapt. And although certain species are more than capable of adjusting to urban life, many are not. When remnants of semi-natural grassland, heathland or woodland are lost to housing or other developments we also lose the vast majority of the wild plants and animals that were living there. What survives is a small subset of the most durable, adaptable and generalist species. If I want to see Marsh Harriers, Skylarks, Yellow Wagtails, Nightingales, or a high diversity of wild flowers, trees or fungi, then I'm not going to head into the nearest town. And if I want to enjoy a bit of downtime in an area where wild animals and plants are the dominant features of the landscape, I'll avoid places where humanity is so clearly in charge. It's great that some species can adapt to urban areas and even thrive among high densities of people, but let's not forget the things that are lost as humanity continues to expand.

A few years ago, an article by David Lindo, the self-styled 'Urban Birder', was full of enthusiasm for urban wildlife and posed the question 'Is urban birding the future?'* It may be for some people – but for me, urban birding is similar to birding in intensively managed farmland. It's about making the best of a bad job. It's about salvaging at least some pleasure from the fact that not everything has been obliterated and some wildlife clings

---

* Lindo, D. (2014) Is urban birding the future? *British Birds* 107: 440–441.

on despite the destructive influence of humanity. The birds (and other animals) we see in urban areas are a welcome distraction from thinking about the diverse range of species that have long since abandoned the place.

CONFLICTS

RECENT ARRIVALS

We're lucky in Britain that the majority of our most widespread and familiar birds are the same native species that have been here with us for thousands of years. Most were present before humans started to have a major impact on the landscape and, with varying levels of success, they have adapted to the changes we have brought about. Other island countries have been less fortunate. In New Zealand, for example, the introduction of invasive predatory mammals has decimated the native bird fauna. Many of the remaining species are now restricted to offshore islands or a few surviving patches of natural forest where they are protected from predators by huge electric fences and the use of poison baits. Unsurprisingly, the control of non-native species in New Zealand is pursued vigorously, to try to save what is left, and tends not to be seen as contentious.

In contrast, the control of non-natives is often highly contentious in Britain, particularly when it comes to birds and mammals. One extreme view is that we should get rid of the lot. None of them has a right to be here, and they inevitably compete with

This chapter is an expanded version of an article first published in the March 2015 issue of *British Birds* (108: 120–121).

native wildlife for food or other resources. Practicalities make eradication of all non-native species impossible, of course, though the development of new technologies such as oral contraception could widen our aspirations in future. At the other extreme are those who say 'live and let live'. If non-natives become established as a result of human intervention then so be it; they have just as much right to an existence as any of our long-established native species.

I'm somewhere in between these two extremes, though leaning more towards getting rid of the lot of them. I could happily live without introduced Pheasants, Red-legged Partridges, Mandarin Ducks, Canada Geese, Egyptian Geese, Ring-necked Parakeets, Mink, Grey Squirrels and Fallow Deer, to name just a few. Biodiversity means more than local species richness. It's about maintaining differences on a larger scale, rather than accepting a similar mix of species across large parts of the globe. I am, however, conscious of some inconsistencies and confusion in my own views. I would, for example, be very reluctant to see the back of the Brown Hare, Rabbit and Little Owl, for reasons that I'm not sure are entirely defensible. As with the control of native wildlife, our views on non-natives are influenced not only by sound evidence and logic but also by our own experiences and personal prejudices.

The Brown Hare is one of my favourite mammals, and one I used to see regularly in the Fens. It has adapted well to intensively managed farmland and often appeared to be the only living thing eking out an existence in some of the more barren arable fields in Cambridgeshire. Although introduced by humans, it has been with us in Britain, sharing our landscapes, for perhaps two thousand years. Is it justifiable to treat it as an honorary native because of this? Maybe, though already I fear the lines are starting to blur. The Rabbit has not been here for quite as long, though long enough to have become deeply integrated into our ecosystems and food webs. It maintains our flower-rich semi-natural grass-lands by keeping the sward short and preventing scrub from getting a foothold. And it provides a vital food source for a whole array of native species including Foxes, Stoats, Buzzards and Red Kites. Removing this non-native mammal from the landscape would have profound effects on many native species – an argument for sparing it, perhaps? Yet a further blurring of the lines.

Little Owls nested in one of the mature Sycamores in our Fenland garden (two non-native species for the price of one). The nest was directly in front of my study, and for several years they provided a welcome distraction from the computer screen through the long breeding season. The sight of the young owls stumbling around in the branches near the nest hole was one of the wildlife highlights of the year. The Little Owl was introduced relatively recently, becoming established following releases in the mid-nineteenth century, and as a pugnacious defender of nest holes it certainly has the potential to impact on native species.* I remember watching violent scraps between the adult owls and the local Stock Doves in the garden in spring, which often ended with feathers from the native species floating down onto the lawn below. Logic suggests that Little Owls should not be welcomed. The only defence I can offer is that the Little Owl's

---

* According to the BTO website (see BirdFacts: www.bto.org/understanding-birds/birdfacts) the Little Owl first bred in Kent in 1879, but releases also took place elsewhere, including in Northamptonshire in central England.

native range includes most of Europe and it is found just across the English Channel on the near continent. The fact that it did not make it to Britain unaided is, it could be argued, a mere quirk of geography and rising sea levels. Had things been slightly different, it might very well have spread here naturally. Is it therefore reasonable to treat it as another honorary native?

The problem with these arguments is that they water down the distinction between natives and non-natives. Everyone's criteria for what should constitute an 'honorary native' will be different. Everyone will have their own favourite species for which they can invoke special pleading. How long ago does an introduction need to have taken place before the species should be accepted? How close does the native range have to be? How entrenched in our ecosystems must a species become before it is spared? I love watching Brown Hares and Little Owls, but is it really tenable to defend them and, at the same time, wish that Grey Squirrels and Ring-necked Parakeets could be eradicated?

My attitude towards the introduced Muntjac deer is especially confused. Logically I accept that this species has no right to be here. It is a recent arrival, becoming established in the early part of the twentieth century following escapes from wildlife parks. Its native range is thousands of kilometres away in southeast China, and it is known to damage native plants and trees in the woodlands it has so successfully invaded. But I have a real soft spot for these animals. When I was growing up in rural Oxfordshire the Muntjac was the only common species of deer in the area. It seemed to fit well into the local landscape and I admired the way it could thrive even in tiny fragments of habitat. When we lived in the Fens, I occasionally saw them along the scrubby verges of the dual carriageways while driving into Peterborough, and close to the edge of the M25 around London. And when I went Badger watching as a child, Muntjac would add a sense of mystery and 'wildness' to the night-time with their strange, barking cries. Sometimes they scared the living daylights out of me. When disturbed at close range they emit an ear-splitting shriek of alarm, shredding the air, before melting away into the trees. To be clear, I would not spare this species as I might spare the Little Owl, Rabbit and Brown Hare. But if we ever find a way to eradicate it, I would be a little sad to see it go. As a result, I sympathise with others who feel the same way about their own favourite non-native animals.

For plants and invertebrates the situation is more complex still. Experts struggle even to agree whether some species are native or introduced, never mind deciding what to do about them. Many plants have been here for so long there is no real choice but to treat them as part of our 'natural' flora. The word 'archaeophyte' is used to denote plants thought to have been introduced in ancient times. Those introduced since 1600 are termed 'neophytes'. These 'recent' arrivals are more likely to be considered as potentially troublesome and as fair game for eradication if they start to have adverse impacts on other species or economic interests. We wage small wars against Himalayan Balsam, Japanese Knotweed and Rhododendron, though some new arrivals are more likely to be tolerated or even welcomed. Buddleja brightens up gardens and patches of waste land in urban areas and its flowers help to keep some of our native butterflies well fed through the summer. Spare a thought too for an entomologist faced with a newly discovered species of flying insect close to the south coast. Has it been introduced? In which case should it be eradicated while the population is still small? Or has it made it across the Channel without human help? In which case, how best should this new addition to the native fauna be managed and protected to help ensure its survival?

In troubled moments I wonder if we can ever hope to develop a coherent approach to non-native species in the midst of such complexity, personal prejudice and widely differing opinions. The consequences of taking no action, however, are considerable. While we are fortunate in comparison with places like New Zealand, the adverse effects of invasive non-natives are well documented, and our vertebrate fauna is becoming more and more dominated by them. The Rabbit, Grey Squirrel, Brown Rat, House Mouse and Muntjac are among our most common and familiar mammals. And Pheasants, Red-legged Partridges and Canada Geese dominate the bird fauna in many lowland landscapes. Pheasants alone make up over 50 per cent of the total bird biomass in lowland Britain, which is unsurprising given that over 40 million of these large birds are released into the wild every year for shooting.* The Ring-necked Parakeet is increasing rapidly, and its requirement for nest holes means that native hole-nesters may lose out as it continues to spread. Already, it is one of the most familiar birds in woodlands and gardens in parts of southeast England. Other non-native birds have either established a foothold in Britain, including Black Swan, Red-crested Pochard and Eagle Owl, or are waiting in the wings for their

---

* Avery, M. (2019) The Common Pheasant in the UK and the potential impacts of an abundant non-native. *British Birds* 112: 372–389.

chance, such as Sacred Ibis and House Crow. Their potential impacts are uncertain, but it seems unrealistic to expect that they will be able to thrive here without adverse impacts on native wildlife.

With limited resources we have no choice but to prioritise efforts to control non-native species, and it seems sensible to concentrate on those that are recent introductions, have the potential for significant impacts on native wildlife (or economic interests) and are well beyond their native range. I have little sympathy for the view that the control of non-native animals is unacceptable, and there is a hint of desperation in some of the arguments put forward to justify that position. Eradicating introduced species is not tantamount to 'ethnic cleansing' as is sometimes suggested, any more than shooting a pigeon or swatting a wasp is 'murder'. Humans and other animals are not the same thing. If we allow the complexities of the arguments to get in the way of action, we risk sleepwalking into a gradual acceptance of more and more non-native species and an ever-growing and ultimately unstoppable erosion of our native wildlife. Not so much 'live and let live' as 'live and let die'.

RESCUING WILDLIFE

I have faced the 'wildlife rescue quandary' many times over the years. The example lodged most clearly in my mind relates to a forlorn-looking Barn Owl nestling found among damp vegetation below its nest, just beyond the boundary of our old garden in the Fens. It made no effort to escape as I approached and so I was faced with the inevitable decision as to whether or not to intervene. It would be easy enough to fetch a ladder from the garage and lift the bedraggled bird back to the safety of its nest. Was that the best thing to do? Or should I accept that this is a wild animal and nature should be allowed to run its course?

It's true, of course, that many of us routinely intervene in the lives of local wildlife by providing food and nest boxes in our gardens, especially for birds. We do so to offer them a helping hand – though in fact it's probably more for our own benefit. It brings birds closer to us so that we can enjoy watching them. I don't go to the trouble of putting food out in local farmland, away from the garden, even though it would be easy enough to do so, and the birds would no doubt appreciate it just as much. In any case, providing food and shelter is one thing. But grabbing hold of a wild animal to rescue it is quite another – a significant escalation in terms of the extent of human intervention involved.

People who spend long hours watching wildlife closely, including wildlife photographers and film-makers, face this sort of situation more often than most. Those who film wildlife may have the added dilemma that the decisions they take are then recorded for public viewing (and judgement). There is the now infamous episode of the BBC's *Springwatch* where a recently fledged Dipper was filmed desperately struggling to avoid drowning in a section of fast-flowing river. It didn't make it, and the BBC was heavily, and I thought unfairly, criticised for not intervening to rescue the bird. It was far from clear whether intervention would even have been feasible, as the bird was moving around rapidly in difficult terrain and would have been tricky to catch. But had a rescue been possible, surely the camera crew were there to film wildlife behaving naturally, including inevitable mishaps, rather than making decisions about whether their subjects should live or die.

Higher up the scale of interventions are those involving more than the brief handling of an animal so it can be moved a short distance to safety. If an animal is injured, ill or underweight, then, in order to save it, a spell in captivity is usually required. It may simply need feeding up, which can be done by anyone with a little knowledge or a willingness to seek advice online. If injury or disease is involved, then specialist knowledge is required, involving either a local vet or one of the many wildlife rehabilitation centres dotted around the country. Every year thousands of young birds are rescued in this way and spend varying periods of time in captivity.

Such interventions are often misguided, because most of these young birds do not need help in the first place. Their parents are nearby, even if they are not in view, and are quite capable of locating their young by homing in on their persistent begging calls. Young Tawny Owls are frequent victims of unnecessary assistance because they leave the nest before they can fly properly and may end up on the ground or a low perch. They are more than capable of scrambling back up to safety within the woodland canopy, but in daylight they often 'freeze' when approached, and the adults are unlikely to make their presence known. It is easy to assume they have been abandoned and need to be whisked off to a rehabilitation centre. But there are, of course, cases where a young bird really has been orphaned or abandoned, and has no chance of survival if left to fend for itself. In that situation, is it right to intervene?

The same sort of issues arise in the case of the Hedgehog. This is an animal that enjoys (or suffers, depending on your point of view) more than its share of human interventions. It's a regular visitor to gardens, even in urban areas, and is one of our most enduringly popular animals. What sets it apart from most mammals (and birds) is the ease with which it can be caught, increasing the opportunity for people to get involved in its wellbeing. The Hedgehog is a well-studied animal. Research has shown that if young animals fail to reach a weight of 600 grams before the onset of cold conditions in late autumn they have little chance of surviving hibernation. This finding has been well publicised and has spawned a whole industry involving animals being picked up and examined in the autumn by enthusiasts. Those below the weight threshold are plucked from the wild, provided with food, and often overwintered indoors before being released in the following spring.

Why am I questioning interventions of this sort? Surely if an animal is found in a situation where its survival chances are poor then it's acceptable to intervene. Some may feel there is even a moral obligation to take action rather than leaving an animal to suffer. I certainly don't have all the answers. But I do have some questions, and they cause me to doubt whether intervention is the best approach – both from a practical and from a philosophical perspective. I'll use the Hedgehog as a case study.

When wildlife ceases to be wild

I value wildlife in large part because of its wildness and its independence from people. Inevitably, wild animals routinely suffer all sorts of traumas such as predation, injury, starvation and disease, and we cannot possibly hope to prevent this from happening. I fear that the more we get involved and the more we interfere, the less 'wild' our wildlife becomes. For me, that devalues it. I want to see Hedgehogs in the garden and in the local countryside because the species has sufficient suitable habitat to get by on its own, not because someone in the village nearby gathers them up in the autumn and releases them from boxes in the garage every spring. Wildlife parks and zoos provide the opportunity to see animals that are dependent on humans for their survival. Wildlife, surely, is a different matter.

Does it work?

By this I mean does it work at the level of helping to conserve local populations? I don't doubt that the survival chances of individual animals can be increased by human intervention, but does that mean the overall population is increased in the long term? I don't think it does, at least not in the majority of cases. Ultimately, our wildlife populations are naturally constrained by the extent of habitat, food and other resources available to them. Providing food for wildlife may increase the available resources and so increase population size. In contrast, taking underweight animals into captivity, boosting their survival chances by feeding them and then releasing them back into the wild is unlikely to make any difference in the long term. There is only so much good-quality habitat and food to go around in any given area. Releasing animals may even increase competition for limited resources by artificially increasing the local population beyond what the local area can support. The effects of this will be unpredictable, depending on a whole range of factors – but one entirely feasible outcome is reduced survival rates in wild Hedgehogs owing to increased competition. More wild animals may end up starving, largely unseen and therefore unreported, but the direct result of human intervention.

For very rare species, where the loss of every individual could reduce the viability of the population, intervention can certainly provide a conservation benefit. But for animals that are still reasonably common and widespread, like the Hedgehog, human intervention contributes little, if anything, to long-term conservation. Sadly, it is estimated that there are only around 1 million Hedgehogs remaining in Britain, with a big drop in numbers over the last few decades. This is against a backdrop of increasing interest from rehabilitation centres but a continued decline in the quality of our countryside and its ability to support the animal.[*]

Is it good for animal welfare?

Human interventions often have animal welfare rather than conservation as the primary motivation. Nobody relishes the prospect of a wild animal starving to death, and if there is a little less suffering among wild Hedgehogs through bringing the weak animals into captivity then surely that can only be a good thing. Yet, as well as the danger of unwittingly increasing levels of competition, there is also the potential suffering involved in being taken into captivity in the first place. This is difficult to judge in most species, and Hedgehogs are not the most expressive of creatures. Perhaps they adapt to temporary captivity rather better than most. But for animals such as Foxes, Badgers, deer and most birds, familiar only with life in the wild and with an in-built healthy fear of human contact, time spent in captivity involves prolonged stress and suffering. Would a relatively quick death in the wild be kinder?

The wider implications

This might appear to be a trivial point, but removing any animal from the wild has consequences beyond the individual involved.

---

[*] Wilson, E. and Wembridge, D. (2018) *The State of Britain's Hedgehogs*. British Hedgehog Preservation Society and the People's Trust for Endangered Species.

An injured, diseased or underweight animal may have little hope of survival, but it has an excellent chance of becoming a decent meal for a predator or scavenger. When it is taken into captivity, we are essentially removing a potential food source for other species. And of course, if a predator is deprived of an easy catch (an animal that was probably destined to die anyway), it will inevitably seek out other targets. If it is successful, then another animal will be killed that may otherwise have survived. If unsuccessful, the predator (or its young) will go hungry.

I also wonder about potential impacts on the process of evolution in the longer term. I'm sure that some underweight Hedgehogs have an excellent set of genes to pass on to the next generation and are struggling only because they were born late in the year or because food is in short supply. But it's likely that underweight animals will include a disproportionately high number of genetically weaker individuals. These animals will be less well adapted to life in the wild and less able to attain the required weight before hibernation. Evolution works by favouring the individuals best placed to survive and breed successfully, and it won't work as efficiently if animals that are less well adapted are rescued, provided with unlimited food, and subsequently returned to the wild. That may seem to be a rather bleak, utilitarian view – but it is important to remember that the wild animals we are so fond of have been moulded over generations by this process.

These are difficult issues, and views will inevitably vary widely. After all, some people shoot healthy Woodpigeons, Rabbits and Foxes as pests, while others rescue injured and sick individuals of the same species and lovingly restore them to full health. The contrast could hardly be greater. I'm advancing these arguments mainly to help justify my own position rather than expecting, necessarily, to change the views of others. I certainly believe that a policy of total non-intervention in respect of sick, unhealthy or weak animals is entirely justifiable, and I think a strong case can be made that intervention brings few, if any, benefits to wildlife. Logically, I think the arguments for non-intervention stack up – though admittedly we are not logical creatures.

To return briefly to that Barn Owl nestling on the ground – despite everything I've just written I couldn't bring myself to walk on by without doing anything. Maybe I could have walked past a young Woodpigeon – but not a young Barn Owl. Out came the ladder, and the bedraggled bird was duly cajoled back to its nest. It re-joined its siblings, cowering in alarm in the darkest corner, furthest from the entrance. Another rescue effort was required a few days later. And several days after that we found the young bird's sorry corpse in the long grass below the nest. With hindsight, it was probably always doomed. All I'd achieved was to unwittingly prolong its suffering.

THE CULTURE OF KILLING

In recent years my former employer, Natural England, has come in for much criticism for licensing the lethal control of Buzzards in order to reduce predation on Pheasants released for shooting. My gut reaction was to share in the general sense of outrage; my initial sympathies were very much with the Buzzard. However, the longer I reflected on the situation, the more I questioned my initial response. I began to think that if the situation was considered logically, taking into account all the other bird control that takes place in Britain, it was difficult to justify these feelings. The protracted debate that ensued got me thinking about the way we appear to value different species (or groups of species) in different ways, and the extent to which tradition and cultural aspects influence our views, albeit often on a subconscious level.

For some people, the killing of any bird for sport or to protect crops, livestock or gamebirds is wrong on moral grounds. While it's not a view I share, I'm envious of its simplicity. It is a straightforward, clear-cut position. And it neatly avoids the complicating influences of culture, tradition and even personal prejudice when it comes to forming a view as to what is, and what is not, acceptable.

For conservation-minded people not opposed to killing on moral grounds, attention usually focuses on whether lethal control (or shooting for sport) will have an impact on the *population* of the animal in question, be that at a national, local or site level. Many species are killed in Britain every year, sometimes in large numbers, with apparently minimal, if any, impacts on populations. Think of the Woodpigeons shot by farmers to protect crops, the Magpies and Carrion Crows killed to protect gamebirds and breeding waders, and the large gulls controlled to protect tern colonies. Then there are the huge numbers of waders, ducks and geese killed by hunters each winter. True, there is sometimes debate about the numbers of birds that can be killed sustainably, but, by and large, we are reassured that populations are not unduly impacted, and the killing of these species tends to receive little media attention.

Traditional practices can be very different in other countries. Here in Britain we are instinctively horrified by the idea of hunters killing large numbers of Blackbirds, Song Thrushes and Skylarks, for example, but this is commonplace and perfectly legal in some European countries. On reflection, it's difficult to find any sound justification for such strong feelings. Why is the shooting of Mallard and Teal for sport acceptable (or at least tolerable) while the killing of Skylarks for the same reason is not? Our strong feelings seem to become instilled in us almost by osmosis, simply by living in a country where there is no recent tradition of hunting these birds.

Talk of instinctive horror brings us back to the Buzzard. The phrase neatly sums up the feelings of many birdwatchers when they learn about the licensed control of this species in England. This strong reaction is presumably not based on concerns for the

Buzzard population. This has increased rapidly in recent decades, to an estimated 61,500–85,000 pairs in Britain according to the latest estimate.* A small number of birds killed under licence will make little difference. Rather, our strong feelings are a purely instinctive reaction to the killing of a bird that has no recent history of legal control in Britain. And, as a bird of prey at the top of the food chain, we perhaps accord it an elevated status. For reasons that are almost impossible to define, it is deemed to be more worthy of protection than, say, a humble gull or a duck or goose. One commentator was quoted as saying that this was 'England's eagle', the implication being that the larger and more impressive the bird, the more outrageous the idea of killing it. This argument has an intrinsic appeal, but surely much the same thing could be said about other species that are killed routinely. A sighting of a Fox or Stoat is always something special, yet both can be controlled legally (with few restrictions) in order to reduce predation of gamebirds or livestock, as well as to protect vulnerable ground-nesting birds.

While it is, of course, legitimate to object to individuals of any species being controlled, it's interesting to try to pin down the reasons behind such opposition. The Buzzard is a popular and impressive bird and has enjoyed full legal protection for many years. Much as with the Skylark, Blackbird and Song Thrush, we have got used to the fact that Buzzards are not hunted in Britain or routinely killed to protect other species. We resent the apparent sudden change in status implied by the issuing of

---

* Woodward, I., Aebischer, N., Burnell, D. *et al.* (2020) Population estimates of birds in Great Britain and the United Kingdom. *British Birds* 113: 69–104.

a licence. This does, however, raise some tricky questions about the way that we apparently value some species more highly than others. Is a Buzzard really worth more to us than a Great Black-backed Gull, a Brent Goose or a Cormorant, all of which have smaller populations in Britain, but are killed regularly under licence without too much of a fuss in the media? Are we saying that a large, impressive bird of prey should be treated differently to these species simply because it is more popular? And, if so, how do we expect this to be reflected in our wildlife legislation?

When a version of this chapter was published a few years ago, it sparked considerable debate among *British Birds* readers.* Most of the contributors to an online discussion fiercely defended the Buzzard. It was suggested that my article had missed a key point, and that people objected to the issuing of the licences not so much because of the species involved but rather because of the purpose for which control was undertaken. One commentator, for example, explained his objection as follows:

> [T]he killing of Buzzards is more about the fact that a licence has been issued to control a native protected bird to favour the commercial interests associated with the non-native Pheasant . . . my objection to the killing of Buzzards isn't based on the way that I value the species at all.

---

* This chapter was developed from an article that first appeared in the September 2013 issue of *British Birds* (106: 490–491).

Despite such a clear statement, I believe the strength of the hostile reaction was indeed because of the species involved. Every year, hundreds of thousands of native birds and mammals are routinely killed in order to protect non-native gamebirds. The birds, including Magpies, Carrion Crows and various large gulls, are all killed under licence. Hundreds of Cormorants are killed each year in order to protect fisheries, including those stocked with non-native Rainbow Trout. While not everyone would agree that this killing is justified, or supported by good evidence, it tends to attract little attention. In contrast, the killing of a handful of Buzzards sparked outrage. The strength of feeling here is surely a reflection of instinctive cultural responses to the bird involved.

A TALE OF TWO RAPTORS

During the past few decades I've been fortunate enough to be involved in conservation efforts involving two of our most enigmatic and impressive birds of prey. Though they share many similarities, their stories are very different. Working with them has involved the full spectrum of emotions, from satisfaction and elation through to disbelief and even despair. The impact of humans on these species provides an especially stark contrast. It's sometimes difficult to believe that the projects involving these two birds are taking place in the same country.

Both birds are strikingly handsome, 'medium-sized' raptors, occupying the middle ground between the smaller Kestrel and Sparrowhawk, and the much larger Golden and White-tailed Eagles. One is a wonderful combination of grace and elegance, with a mastery of the air unrivalled by any other bird of prey. It spends long hours floating slowly and effortlessly over the countryside, and increasingly over villages and towns, but has an impressive turn of speed and supreme manoeuvrability when the need arises. The other bird also spends long periods on the wing but, in contrast, tends to hug the contours of the land, cruising just a few metres above the ground. While one spends most of its time high overhead on the lookout for animal carrion, the other is an ambush predator, constantly alert to hunting opportunities and the chance to snatch a pipit, lark, vole . . . or even a grouse.

In terms of population trends, the two are poles apart. The Red Kite is a conservation success story. It has recovered from the brink of extinction in Britain, and following its reintroduction to many different areas it is increasing and spreading rapidly. It is now common in parts of the country and well on the way to full restoration as one of our most widespread and familiar raptors. The Hen Harrier has not been so fortunate. At the same time as the Red Kite has made its return, so the Hen Harrier has dwindled and faded from many of its former haunts. Reasonable numbers are still present in parts of Scotland and Wales, but in England, despite the hint of an upturn in recent years, only nineteen pairs nested in 2020.

Not surprisingly, given their respective stories, there are major contrasts in the public perception of these birds. The Red Kite is hugely, if not universally, popular. Most people with even a passing interest in wildlife know what it looks like and have had the opportunity to watch it in Britain. In areas where it has become common, it has been welcomed back with open arms and people take great pleasure in being able to watch this elegant raptor in their local countryside. It mostly eats carrion and poses little threat to livestock or gamebirds. There have been a few grumbles about the predation of songbirds and wader chicks, but while the Red Kite is not averse to taking live prey from time to time, it offers no real threat to the populations of other birds. Its scavenging habits, lack of fear of humans and ability to snatch up food from the most enclosed of spaces mean that it can be attracted to village gardens with scraps of meat. This has become common practice in places, and although not everyone thinks it's a good idea, it certainly provides spectacular close-up views, and only adds to the bird's appeal. Some village gardens are now visited by twenty or more kites on a daily basis, providing a wildlife spectacle that would have been unimaginable in England just a few years ago.*

In comparison, the Hen Harrier struggles to get a look in. It's not that it's a bad-looking bird; the ghostly pale adult males are stunning. But when it comes to popularity, it has two major problems. One is that it shuns the limelight. It breeds (when it gets a chance) on remote areas of upland moorland where birdwatchers are thin on the ground. And although it's far more widely dispersed in winter, it favours wide open expanses such as saltmarsh, heathland, grassland and arable farmland. This is not a bird you can lure into your garden with a few scraps, nor one that will hang in droves over your village allowing you to watch at your leisure. Views of the Hen Harrier tend to be hard-won, distant, short-lived and perhaps, for the non-birdwatcher, rather uninspiring. In contrast to the Red Kite, most people with a casual interest in wildlife would have difficulty identifying a Hen Harrier and have probably yet to see one. It's hard to care about a bird if you are not familiar with it, and the lack of public appreciation does it no favours when it comes to the second major problem: its fondness for heather moorland and for the highly prized Red Grouse that live there. Grouse shooting is big business these days, and a bird that makes its living by quartering the moors, with killing on its mind, does not endear itself to moorland gamekeepers. Even when not eating grouse it is still

---

* See discussion about feeding Red Kites in the next chapter.

an unwelcome presence through its reputation for 'spooking' them on shoot days, making it difficult to drive them over the patiently waiting line of guns.

My involvement with these two species also provides a contrasting picture. With the Red Kite I was directly involved in some of the hands-on work in England. Back in the 1990s I was part of a small team that visited central Spain to bring back young kites for release in Rockingham Forest, Northamptonshire. I was involved in monitoring them from their first uncertain flights into the wild, through pairing up and breeding, and their resulting contribution to a growing population. This allowed me to develop a real understanding of the species. It also resulted in a deep connection with it, one that will stay with me for the rest of my life. Although I haven't done any serious fieldwork involving Red Kites in recent years, I still keep in close touch with progress. Whenever a new report is published dealing with the status or ecology of birds in Britain, the Red Kite is always the bird I turn to first. And when the wrapping is impatiently torn from a new natural history book, I quickly check the index to see whether the Red Kite gets a mention.

I haven't done much hands-on work with Hen Harriers and have spent little time studying them in the field. Instead, I have spent long hours in offices, meeting rooms and on the end of a phone, playing a small part in setting up conservation projects and, subsequently, helping to decide what to do with the results. As a result, I'm (thankfully) a little more detached when it comes to the Hen Harrier, though it's still a bird I love to see. Perhaps ironically, it's a bird I do see more often than the Red Kite following our move to the southwest of England. They are regular, if infrequent, winter visitors in this area and every so often I'll encounter one drifting across the fields when I'm out walking, especially on visits to Dartmoor, about an hour's drive from the house. The Hen Harrier's foraging flight can seem rather aimless and half-hearted, almost as if it is going through the motions as it drifts back and forth across the ground. Only when something is flushed does its true purpose become apparent – as the bird stalls in the air, twists and folds its wings in one movement, and dives down towards the ground, long legs outstretched in anticipation of a meal.

I've been lucky enough to be shown around some of the few remaining Hen Harrier breeding sites in northern England by Stephen Murphy, Natural England's long-standing (and long-suffering) Hen Harrier expert. He has, somehow, managed to maintain his inspiring and infectious enthusiasm while studying this bird, despite the heavy toll of persecution and the perilously small pool of birds available to work with. From my hands-on involvement with the Red Kite, I understand the connection he has with the Hen Harrier, and the utter frustration and despair he must feel trying to save a bird reduced to a fraction of its former population in England. When discussing the latest satellite-tagged bird to go missing from the radar or yet another breeding attempt that has failed in suspicious circumstances, I can hear it in his voice.*

If you think about the Red Kite you might be tempted to pat yourself on the back on behalf of humanity, and reflect on how

---

* For the full, sorry story of the decline of the Hen Harrier and its relationship with driven grouse shooting see Avery, M. (2019) *Inglorious: Conflict in the Uplands.* Bloomsbury, London.

enlightened we are these days. Long-term persecution removed this species (along with many others) from most of Britain. That it has now been restored not only shows commitment and determination from those involved, but is also testament to the significantly changed attitudes of people living and working in the countryside. Although there are still persecution incidents in the lowlands where Red Kites are making their comeback, these are now the exception rather than the rule, and populations in most areas have been able to flourish. Only in release areas close to the uplands is the kite still struggling to become established, reflecting the higher levels of persecution associated with driven grouse shooting. There are now several thousand pairs of kites in the Chilterns but only around 100 pairs on the Black Isle, in northern Scotland, where persecution remains a major problem.

That brings us back to the Hen Harrier, a bird that is reliant on the uplands for its breeding sites. When you consider the remnant population in England, clinging on desperately against an onslaught of persecution, you may think we deserve a kick up the backside rather than a pat on the back. The Red Kite was lost from England as far back as the 1860s as a direct result of the sustained human persecution that was typical of the age. It seems scarcely believable that we could lose the Hen Harrier from England for the very same reason, in the early decades of the twenty-first century.

MEDDLING WITH WILDLIFE

Most birds in Britain benefit from human interventions of one kind or another. These measures are largely indirect and uncontentious, involving the restoration or appropriate management of suitable habitat. Nature reserve managers essentially choose the suite of species they wish to cater for. A large reedbed may support a healthy population of Marsh Harriers, Bitterns and Bearded Tits, as well as the more numerous Reed and Sedge Warblers. But, left unmanaged, reed-litter accumulates, the site starts to dry out, bushes begin to appear, and the balance shifts towards birds of scrub and young woodland. Equally, a reserve with dense scrub supporting high densities of warblers and Nightingales will gradually revert to more mature woodland if left unmanaged, and again the suite of species present will after. Site managers are constantly intervening to prevent such changes from taking place.

Conservationists also undertake more direct measures that do not relate solely to habitat management. At one end of the scale this can be something as simple as the provision of food or artificial nest sites, or it may involve the active control of competitors or predators in order to favour a chosen species. At the other end of the scale are reintroduction projects (considered in the next chapter), where intervention extends to physically moving birds from one place to another, or the release of birds bred in captivity. The following examples give a flavour of the range of interventions undertaken. As an ornithologist, I find myself defaulting naturally to bird examples, but a similar range of interventions apply to other groups. Conservation involves a lot of meddling with wildlife.

Artificial nests

The provision of nest boxes or platforms in order to compensate for a paucity of natural nest sites is a conservation measure familiar to everyone. Boxes are often installed in gardens to attract common birds. They provide additional nest sites and they allow us to enjoy the comings and goings of the adults as they try to rear the next generation of young birds.

Even when natural sites are available, boxes can still have a positive effect if they offer security from predators of eggs or young. Where there is a shortage of natural sites, boxes can significantly increase the density of breeding birds. In extreme cases, the use of nest boxes encourages birds that would otherwise not be present in an area because of an absence of natural sites. In one Swedish birch forest, the provision of boxes resulted in a 24-fold increase in the density of Pied Flycatchers. The authors of the study acknowledged that they had effectively 'introduced' the Pied Flycatcher to this wood.* Barn Owls in treeless parts

---

* Enemar, A. and Sjöstrand, B. (1972) Effects of the introduction of Pied Flycatchers on the composition of a passerine bird community. *Ornis Scandinavica* 3: 79–89.

of as the world, whether that is the East Anglian Fens or the edge of a desert in the Middle East, are able to thrive only because of the extensive network of pole-mounted nest boxes that have been provided for them. Of course, changes that directly benefit one species may have the opposite effect on its competitors or its prey, something that conservationists need to keep in mind. A wood with lots of nest boxes for Blue and Great Tits may become a more challenging place for the declining Marsh Tit to live. They are less likely to use the boxes, and may face stiffer competition for food from higher numbers of the other species.*

Supplementary feeding

The use of artificial food to help birds has a long history and involves millions of people in Britain. Huge amounts of food are provided in gardens, and this helps sustain birds that would otherwise struggle, especially in harsh winters. In addition, the RSPB and others have increasingly adopted supplementary feeding as a conservation measure away from gardens, often making the most of the opportunity to provide people with spectacular close-up views of birds. In winter, waste potatoes and grain are fed daily to Whooper and Bewick's Swans at the Wildfowl & Wetlands Trust reserve on the Ouse Washes in Norfolk. The food is placed in front of the main hide so that visitors can enjoy the spectacle. Red Kites are given butchers'

* Broughton, R. K. and Hinsley, S. A. (2015) The ecology and conservation of the Marsh Tit in Britain. *British Birds* 108: 12–28.

offcuts at organised feeding stations in Britain, and Tree Sparrows benefit from seed provided close to nest boxes on nature reserves trying to encourage this species. In winter, seed-eating finches and sparrows also benefit from feeding stations established by conservation-minded farmers to replace food sources that have been lost from our intensively farmed landscapes.

Supplementary feeding can also be used to help keep birds away from harmful food sources. A feeding programme for White-tailed Eagles in Sweden was started because of concerns about low breeding productivity as a result of DDT and other pesticides, ingested when they foraged on natural prey. Around 100 feeding stations were set up, providing 150 tonnes of uncontaminated meat each winter, helping to ensure the population survived until pesticide levels had fallen.* Similar measures have been established for various vultures in Europe and the perilously rare California Condor, at risk from lead ammunition when scavenging on the remains of animals killed by hunters.†

Severe winters add to the pressures on vulnerable bird populations, and supplementary feeding programmes have been instigated for birds not typically associated with hand-outs. The Dartford Warbler, one of only two warblers whose entire British population remains in this country for the winter (the other being Cetti's Warbler), is known to be vulnerable to severe weather. The population has crashed in the past during harsh winters, and so mealworms have been provided for them on

---

* Helander, B., Bignert, A. and Asplund, L. (2008) Using raptors as environmental sentinels: monitoring the White-tailed Eagle in Sweden. *AMBIO* 37: 425–431.

† Snyder, N. and Snyder, H. (2000) *The California Condor: A Saga of Natural History and Conservation.* Academic Press, London.

heathland nature reserves to help improve survival rates. Even the reclusive Bittern has received hand-outs. Staff at several reserves have provided dead sprats to help compensate for the fact that natural food is difficult to obtain during spells of freezing weather.

As with the provision of nest boxes, feeding can favour certain species over others and result in unintended consequences that may cause problems. The feeding of Red Kites in gardens has become especially contentious in recent years. It can attract less-welcome species such as corvids and rats, and it may annoy neighbours who are not all going to be happy with large numbers of birds of prey swooping menacingly overhead on a daily basis. Some people believe that these birds should be left to forage naturally rather than provisioned with scraps. Others point out that Red Kites have always been opportunist scavengers, regularly taking advantage of human hand-outs. We feed other birds in our gardens, it is argued, so why not feed Red Kites?

Reducing predators and competitors

Perhaps the most familiar example here is the control of non-native predators in order to assist vulnerable bird populations. Introduced mammals have caused extensive problems around the world, particularly on seabird islands where birds depend on the absence of ground predators. They have no defence against the rats, cats, mink and even tree snakes that have caused population crashes and local extinctions following their intro-duction to predator-free islands around the world. In the Western Isles of Scotland, introduced Hedgehogs have caused declines in ground-nesting waders including Dunlin, Redshank, Snipe and Lapwing, through the predation of eggs. Control programmes are usually the only effective solution to the problem, and they have been widely employed.

A more unusual example involves the introduced Ruddy Duck in Britain. Following the first releases of this North American species in the 1950s, a sizeable population became established. Birds from Britain dispersed and small numbers reached Spain, where interbreeding with the globally threatened White-headed Duck presented a serious threat. In order to tackle the problem, the UK government launched a Ruddy Duck eradication programme in 2005 which has succeeded in reducing the population to just a handful of birds.

It's not only introduced species that cause problems. Rare and declining ground-nesting birds are at risk from a wide range of generalist native predators, including Foxes, Stoats and corvids such as the Carrion Crow. Predation is not a problem for species with healthy, resilient populations occupying extensive areas of good-quality nesting habitat. But for rare species, restricted to small, fragmented patches of habitat, it can cause major problems. If predators cannot be fully excluded by fences (a significant intervention in its own right), then reserve managers may feel obliged to resort to lethal control.

These choices are contentious, and reflect the difficult decisions that conservationists are often faced with. Hedgehogs, Foxes and even Ruddy Ducks have their supporters, who resent the idea that they should be killed in order to protect other species. Tensions run especially high when it comes to birds of prey, with a fierce debate raging about the extent to which they impact on other wildlife. There are no easy decisions but one thing is clear: in a country where habitats and wildlife populations are fragmented, it is a constant struggle to balance the needs of all our wildlife. Allowing predators and competitors to thrive unchecked will not always be possible without accepting reductions (or even the complete loss) of other species. A certain amount of meddling will always be required.

MOVING THINGS AROUND

The range of management techniques described in the previous chapter are challenging and involve measures not welcomed by everyone. Opinions are perhaps more polarised still when it comes to a very specific form of intervention, which involves moving a species from one place to another in order to further its conservation. Here the choices become starker and the role played by direct human intervention even more obvious. For some people, this is a step too far; for them it simply feels wrong when an animal or plant is present in an area only because it has been put there by humans.

Despite such concerns, reintroduction is increasingly used as a conservation technique for a wide range of species. Groups that are easy to handle, such as butterflies, amphibians, reptiles and plants, get moved around so often that their 'natural' distributions are increasingly difficult to determine. If Great Crested Newts or Purple Emperors (two commonly moved species) are found at a new site then it may not be clear whether they reached it through natural spread or as a result of direct human intervention. For species with legal protection, clandestine reintroductions are inevitably shrouded in secrecy, adding to the risk of confusion. The true 'natural' distribution of many animals (and even some plants) is becoming increasingly obscure.

Thankfully, the picture is rarely so confused with birds and mammals, mainly because it's more difficult to catch them so that they can be carted off to a new location. Birdwatchers have often pondered the peculiar distribution of the Crested Tit, a bird common in all kinds of woodland on the continent but, in Britain, restricted to the pine forests of the Scottish Highlands. If their eggs hatched into chicks that were robust and easy to transport, someone would surely by now have introduced a few into an English wood. Fascinating as such an experiment would be, I'm glad it hasn't happened and I'm glad that the distribution of most native birds still reflects natural dispersal patterns rather than translocations by humans.

Nonetheless, there has been a steady increase in organised reintroduction projects for birds, aimed at restoring species extinct in Britain or lost from large parts of their former range. The White-tailed Eagle was the pioneer, with releases starting in Scotland in 1975. Since then there have been projects involving the Red Kite, Osprey, White-tailed Eagle (in England this time), Corncrake, Crane, Great Bustard and Cirl Bunting. These projects involve bringing in young birds (or less often eggs) from overseas, or the translocation of birds within Britain. By and large they have been successful, though the outcome remains uncertain for Corncrakes on the Nene Washes in Cambridgeshire, and Great Bustards on Salisbury Plain. Both birds have started to breed in the wild but have yet to establish self-sustaining populations. Across the Irish Sea there have been releases of Red Kites, White-tailed Eagles and Golden Eagles, all of which appear well on their way to becoming re-established. On the mammal front, there have been attempts to bring back the Beaver through a combination of organised and covert releases. There have also been translocations within Britain to help increase the distribution of Water Voles, Dormice, Pine Martens, Red Squirrels and Otters, among others.

Birds and mammals are popular groups, and reintroduction projects involving them have a high public profile. The rights and wrongs are fiercely debated, even among conservationists. Some people feel uncomfortable with a species being, as they see it, excessively manipulated by humans, even when the aim is to restore it to its former range. Animals handled by humans and then released, at a place of our choosing, become less 'wild' in the eyes of some commentators. As Peter Marren so eloquently put it,

> reared animals become property . . . they are part of *our* grand design, not nature's. The friendliest cock-sparrow that enters our gardens for the opportunities it finds there is wilder than the fiercest cage-reared eagle.*

If released birds carry monitoring aids such as wing-tags or radio-transmitters, the perceived loss of 'wildness' is increased. For many people (for me too), wildlife watching is partly a way of escaping from everyday concerns, a welcome respite from the rigours of life in a human-dominated world. Wildlife offers such an escape because it survives, by and large, on its own terms, despite the huge impacts of human activity all around us.

---

* Marren, P. (2002) Unnatural selection. *The Independent*, 30 September 2002.

Although we may help birds by providing food and nest boxes, or by managing nature reserves, the birds themselves choose whether or not to make use of these opportunities. In contrast, when birds are reintroduced, they are present only because specific choices have been made for them by people. Humans are firmly in control.

Those involved in reintroductions may consider this viewpoint to be pedantic, unhelpful and even obstructive. But I think it's an understandable reaction and one that deserves to be taken seriously. Rather than criticising such views, what is needed is reassurance. And one source of reassurance is the fact that reintroductions actually involve only a small amount of human intervention, when compared to other conservation approaches, *provided a long-term view is taken*. In the mid-1990s, the majority of Red Kites in England and Scotland were released birds sporting their ugly plastic wing-tags, and they could be seen only in the small areas specifically chosen as release sites. But, over the past thirty years, they have reoccupied increasingly large areas through natural spread. The population is now dominated by wild-bred birds, free of human adornments. Birds pair up and settle in new areas of their own volition, selecting nest sites and feeding areas according to their own innate preferences, rather than decisions taken by people. In so doing, they are surely regaining the wildness that may not have been present in the early stages of the release projects. They are, once again, becoming a familiar, natural and accepted part of our countryside.

If you remain unconvinced, it's worth thinking about some of the birds re-established in Britain long ago. How many of us pause to think about the role played by people when watching a Capercaillie in the Scottish Highlands? We may be fully aware that the species is present only because, following extinction, birds were released by humans in the nineteenth century. But sufficient time has passed for this not to intrude on our enjoyment of the spectacle. The Little Owl provides a further example, albeit one that involves an introduced species rather than a reintroduction. We have all grown up with Little Owls in the countryside, and it is now a familiar bird across large parts of the country. It's all too easy to forget that it is only present because of choices made by humans a little over 150 years ago.

There is another reason why reintroductions should not be thought of as 'unnatural'. We must not forget the direct role played by humans in the loss of the species in the first place. Red Kites and White-tailed Eagles were systematically eliminated because of concerns about their impacts on gamebirds and livestock. In reintroducing them, conservationists are doing the exact opposite of what is sometimes claimed. They are attempting to restore a more natural situation. They are bringing back birds which, without past human interference, would already be present as a natural part of the countryside. These days, well-organised reintroductions take place only following extensive consultations with local people in the proposed release area. No such public consultations were ever undertaken prior to the extermination of the species. This is an obvious point but one I'd not fully considered until I read John Love's views in his book about the White-tailed Eagle reintroduction.* Having thought about it more, I wonder where we would be now if more of our predators

---

* Love, J. (2013) *A Saga of Sea Eagles.* Whittles Publishing, Dunbeath.

had been successfully eliminated by unconsented persecution in the past. Perhaps I'm wrong, but I don't think many gamekeepers or farmers today would wish to see Buzzards, Foxes, Stoats and Badgers completely eradicated from Britain, however much they may grumble about them. And yet if persecution in the past had removed them, I'm sure any proposal to bring them back would be subject to fierce opposition.

My views on reintroductions have changed over the years. I've become something of a convert, albeit with the caveat that it should be used as a last resort, only when less intrusive interventions are not feasible. Projects undertaken when natural recolonisation could achieve much the same outcome within a reasonable period are, I think, counterproductive. They may be conceived with publicity, rather than conservation, as the primary purpose. And they take away some of the joy that comes from allowing natural processes to play out wherever possible.

Properly organised reintroductions are undoubtedly expensive. They require funding for release pens, monitoring equipment and veterinary checks, in addition to the costs of collecting and transporting the animals from one place to another, or costs associated with captive breeding. These tasks and post-release monitoring are also labour-intensive. Such investments of time and resources must be made over a number of years to ensure that sufficient animals are released to establish a viable population. Are these high costs justified when they are directed at the restoration of just a single species, especially considering that resources for conservation work are far from limitless? Would the money be better spent, for example, on the acquisition of valuable wildlife habitat, the establishment of nature reserves, or the ongoing management work required to maintain the habitats and wildlife present on existing reserves?

There will always be debate about how best to use scarce resources. The apparent cherry-picking of the highest-profile, most spectacular or 'sexiest' species for reintroduction may, understandably, raise eyebrows. Do we really want to live in a world where only animals that enjoy popular appeal are worthy of our attention and resources? Nonetheless, it is hard to blame conservation organisations for choosing to focus on such a narrow range of species. Reintroductions will only succeed if sufficient funding can be raised, and this is more likely for projects involving high-profile species. Headline-grabbing animals such as the Lynx, Wildcat, Beaver and large raptors will probably always get more than their fair share of attention.

When considering whether reintroductions provide value for money it's important to take account of the full range of benefits they provide. Although the focus is, quite rightly, on the restoration of the species in question, this is by no means the whole story. For one thing, high-profile reintroductions help to encourage a greater interest in wildlife. Reintroduced Red Kites have done just that, even among people who normally pay little attention to the natural world. There is a real thirst for information about this new addition to the local countryside. When problems arise, such as accidental poisoning or illegal persecution, local support is invaluable in trying to address them. Project funds have been used to help tackle these threats, for example by promoting alternative, safer forms of pest control. This bene-fits Red Kites but, crucially, it also improves conditions for a range of other species affected by the same problems. With reintroduced Cirl Buntings and Corncrakes, the extent and appro-priate management of suitable habitat is a key factor. Get the habitat right for these birds, and it will also be suitable for a wide range of other species. To fall back on the conservation jargon, these species are acting as 'flagships', and money spent on their reintroduction should be seen in that context.

Finally, it is worth emphasising that reintroductions are only appropriate for a small number of species. Most animals (birds especially) are mobile enough to naturally recolonise areas from which they have been lost, providing that sufficient habitat is available and we are prepared to exercise a little patience. The best (and the cheapest) reintroductions are those that never need to occur.

WILD PLACES

THE PURSUIT OF WILDNESS

I retain strong memories of a day out, a few years ago, that I spent with my two children, Ali and Ben. During the drive from home I could already sense some of the likely frustrations that lay ahead. They started for real in the car park – pay and display, of course, and as usual I didn't have the correct change. Five minutes (and one helpful lady) later, we were on our way again. The queue to pay the entrance fee was thankfully not too long despite the school holidays, though the business of paying was prolonged by a series of questions about annual passes and a membership scheme – all declined, several times, slightly more tersely with each repetition. There was a further delay as we were handed a detailed map and then given coloured plastic wristbands to prove we had paid. I imagine it was a different colour for each day of the week. Today's was bright, lurid pink.

Safely inside, we set about trying to find the site's star attraction. The map was a good start. And the immaculately manicured paths were flanked by numerous information boards giving further helpful information, as well as strict instructions to keep to the path at all times. It was one of the volunteers dotted around the site who eventually provided the directions we needed, though not before he had quizzed us again about the membership scheme. This was starting to feel like hard work, and we were still on the wrong side of the site. Ten minutes later we were finally in the right place and we joined a loose group of perhaps thirty people, hopefully scouring the path-side vegetation. 'How long have you been looking?' I ventured. 'Almost an hour, nothing yet,' came the deflating reply.

We didn't manage to connect with the star attraction that day. The Adders we'd come to see on this nature reserve eluded us and, in a way, I'm relieved. I hope that when my children see this enigmatic animal for the first time we will not have had to pay for the experience and we will not have followed dozens of other people along purpose-built pathways to a well-known, staked-out location. I hope that when it finally happens, they will come away with a sense of awe and wonder at the wild creatures that can still be chanced upon in this country.

Almost all our remaining 'wild' places have been altered in some way by humans. You might think that areas specifically set aside for wildlife in nature reserves would be an exception – but, if anything, the levels of intervention are especially high in such places. Conservation managers fight an endless battle to prevent heathlands and grasslands from turning into woodland, and 'scrub-bashing' is a familiar task for conservation volunteers. Reedbeds too are prone to invasion by scrub, and it is held at bay by keeping water levels artificially high and through the use of machinery to periodically scrape away the accumulated layer of reed-litter. Woodland is also heavily modified by conservation managers. Blocks of trees are cut back to encourage the coppice regrowth favoured by breeding warblers, and to allow light to reach shade-averse plants and their dependent butterflies on the forest floor. Woodland that has not been managed in this way is said by conservationists to have been 'neglected', which seems an odd choice of word for an area of wildlife habitat that has been left to nature.

If we wish to maintain a wide range of habitats and the varied species they support, we have no choice but to intervene on a regular basis. Leaving everything to nature is not really an option for our small surviving patches of high-quality wildlife habitat. Not unless we are willing to sacrifice our much-loved heaths and flower-rich chalk grasslands, together with their Nightjars, Stone-curlews, Sand Lizards and Smooth Snakes. If we fail to maintain reedbeds, we will lose our breeding Bitterns, Bearded Tits and Marsh Harriers. And in woodland there are many species, from birds to butterflies, which depend on the opening up of the canopy, the associated increase in light levels and the dense regrowth of coppice stools. An artificial patchwork of different-aged blocks of trees, created through management, provides a wider range of habitats and supports a higher diversity of wildlife than a more uniform area of 'neglected' woodland.

The management required to maintain good habitat does not, in itself, detract too much from the wildlife, unless of course you're unlucky enough to visit on a day when the chainsaws and diggers are out in force. On many reserves, though, escape from the all-pervading influence of humans is not really an option. All too often, our reserves can feel more like theme parks than wild places. When a new site is acquired as a nature reserve, the first act of management is often to reduce the area of habitat a little in order to ensure that human visitors are properly catered for. New buildings spring up. They take up space (and habitat), and while some are sensitively blended into the landscape, others jut above the skyline, visible for miles around. Tower hides are increasingly popular, and while they provide visitors with commanding views over the landscape, they dominate the whole area, potent symbols of the extent to which humans are in control. Much the same can be said for the cafes and visitor centres installed on our busier reserves.

Further habitat may be lost in order to ensure that all parts of the site are accessible. Visitors are raised safely above the ground on specially constructed boardwalks, spared from having to make contact with the damp ground beneath. Even on drier sites there will be a network of artificial tracks and paths; they are there to provide assistance for humans rather than habitat for wildlife, although they do help to reduce disturbance to sensitive habitats. For times when watching the wildlife is insufficient to hold the attention, additional artificial features may be added. White-plastic information boards spring up, letting people know about the things they might see or offering instructions to ensure that no-one gets lost, strays from the path or, heaven forbid, starts picking the flowers or sampling the berries.

If people are well catered for in terms of refreshments and shelter, the same is true for the wild animals. The most pampered species are no longer expected to subsist on natural food or find natural places to nest or roost. Bird and bat boxes adorn the trees, and artificial food, some of it flown in from the tropics, is provided in abundance on bird tables and in feeders. Handy, shingle-covered platforms are installed on lakes for the terns. Ground-nesting birds at high risk of predation are protected with wire cages or surrounded by predator-proof electric fences so that they can breed undisturbed.

As on the day when we were searching for Adders, I feel a little cheated when visiting these places – cheated of the sense of escapism and of the satisfaction that comes from exploring a wild area on my own terms. Yet despite the grudging tones (exaggerated a little for effect), I don't have an inherent objection to this type of nature reserve. The majority of visitors appreciate all the information and advice on offer, can live with the sales pitch, and are pleased that viewing opportunities are enhanced by hides, walkways and feeding stations. People vote with their feet, and the cafes and shops are well used. They help raise money and recruit members for a very worthy cause. Reserves like this attract large numbers of people who would not otherwise spend much time in the countryside where they can see, and hopefully come to care about, wildlife. I'm a regular visitor to well-managed nature reserves and have had plenty of stunning, close-up views of animals that would not have been so easy to attain in wilder places. This is partly because many creatures become habituated to large numbers of visitors and learn that, on a nature reserve, humans do not represent a significant threat.

What *would* concern me is if nature reserves were the only option for watching wildlife. Could that happen? The signs are not encouraging. Already, in the most heavily developed parts of the country, most of the remaining areas with abundant wildlife are in nature reserves, and it is difficult to escape from human influence and the theme-park version of wildlife watching. Away from the coast, my favourite places for watching wildlife in Britain are patches of 'neglected' woodland, where signs of previous human interventions have long since faded into the background. These sites are far from truly natural, but they *feel* natural and wild. The young trees grow where they have seeded themselves, and the tangle of vegetation and fallen branches can make it challenging to find a way through. The wild animals, as well as any human visitors, must fend for themselves rather than relying on hand-outs. These woodlands support fewer species than sites subject to carefully planned conservation management, but they provide a welcome escape from a world dominated by humanity. I would hate to lose them, either through felling for development, or through enhanced management and conversion into nature reserves.

SEABIRDS AT SEA

After various spells of voluntary work and a few short-term contracts, my first 'proper' job in conservation was working for the Seabirds at Sea team at the old Nature Conservancy Council. I spent two years there between 1990 and 1992, based at their office in Aberdeen. The bulk of the work involved offshore surveys to improve our understanding of how seabirds use the marine environment throughout the year. Mostly this was carried out from ships, though to obtain good coverage close to shore there was also a programme of aerial surveys. About 30 per cent of my time was spent in the 'field', with the rest in the office helping to analyse the data collected. It was a fantastic introduction to the world of bird surveying and conservation, though I found the surveys themselves rather challenging. In fact, they involved a remarkably varied set of experiences; some were frustrating, depressing, even soul-destroying, while others were uplifting and exhilarating.

One major problem I had to contend with was seasickness. I suffered on almost all the long-haul ship-based surveys. For the first couple of days after the onset of windy weather I'd be confined to my cabin, spending most of the time laid flat-out on the bed. After a day or so the feeling would start to lessen, and by the end of day two I was usually able to return to what I was supposed to be doing: recording seabird activity. Going through the initial bout of sickness provided immunity from any further spells of bad weather later in the trip, unless they were especially severe. Despite knowing from experience that the feelings would pass, I can't overstate the sense of despair that results from lying on a bunk in a tiny cabin, feeling the ship constantly rise and fall, and listening to the sound of the hull slamming down, repeatedly, into the waves, all the time knowing that we would not be back within sight of dry land for another two weeks.

Not quite so desperate, but also difficult to deal with, were the long periods standing on the bridge of the ship, staring out over a cold, grey sea and seeing almost no seabirds. In some areas, especially well offshore, this could be the situation for hours at a time, with nothing to see and nothing to record. During these periods even a single Herring Gull, Fulmar or Kittiwake would be a cause for minor celebration. Such long spells of inactivity could make the job seem utterly pointless, though of course that was far from true. Finding the important places for seabirds was only possible by looking for contrasts between areas with few birds and areas with notable concentrations. Nonetheless, when a day's worth of seabirds fitted easily onto a single sheet of paper it was difficult to derive much job satisfaction from the task at hand.

In winter, the numbing effects of severely cold weather were not to be underestimated. Surveying involved standing high up on the bridge, at the front of the ship, so that birds on the water could be seen before they took evasive action. Heading into the wind in cold conditions meant being blasted by an unbroken stream of freezing air for hours on end. In unsettled weather that air might be full of rain, sleet or snow, flung horizontally by the wind and stinging exposed flesh. In rough seas there was the added menace of icy sea spray, thrown up and onto the bridge as the bow of the ship crashed into each wave. Once cold had set in there was not much chance to warm up until the end of each long session. The fact that the warm, comfortable wheelhouse was usually just a few metres away, full of warm, comfortable members of the ship's crew, sipping coffee, only added to the feeling of hardship.

But there were also days when such trials and tribulations were a distant memory and it seemed scarcely believable I was being paid for work that was so enjoyable and stimulating. Days when the sun shone, the sea was flat and glassy, and the ship was moving through an area with huge, diverse assemblages of seabirds. Days when Common or White-beaked Dolphins approached the ship and spent time riding on the bow-wave just a few metres from where I was standing. One particular day in early September, not far from the Isles of Scilly, an adult Sabine's Gull flew alongside the ship for thirty minutes, at times hanging in the updrafts, so close to me that faint white flecks in an otherwise dark hood could be picked out with the naked eye. The fact that one of these good days could easily follow a series of dull and uninspiring ones made the whole experience bearable; even on the bad days I knew that things could rapidly improve.

One memorable late-summer survey involved travelling through remote parts of the North Sea about halfway between the Faroe Islands and Norway, well north of Shetland. Despite the apparent vastness and emptiness of the ocean, even out here human activity has a major impact on wildlife. For hours and hours nothing at all would be visible from one horizon to the other, except perhaps the odd lone Fulmar or Kittiwake. Vast expanses of sea with no human presence, no human structures or artefacts, and almost no birds. It felt like a wilderness of sorts, though more akin to a desert than a rainforest, given the almost total absence of visible wildlife. Then, a speck in the distance up ahead would gradually resolve itself into the shape of a fishing boat as we steamed towards it. On days when the sea was calm, only the top portion of a distant vessel, perhaps just the tip of the mast, would be visible at first – a flat sea revealing that we inhabit a round earth. As the distance diminished, and the outline of the boat became more obvious, the number of seabirds would start to increase. When we were within a few kilometres of a boat there would often be seabirds everywhere, heavily concentrated around the fishing vessel itself, especially if it was hauling in its nets or processing fish on board, with the inevitable waste discarded over the side.

As with garden birds and bird feeders, not all species of seabird take advantage of free food from fishing boats. North of Shetland the birds taking the hand-outs included thousands of Fulmars, Storm Petrels, Gannets, Great Skuas and at least six different species of gull. The near absence of these species from most of the seascape, coupled with high concentrations close to fishing boats, showed that even out here, hundreds of kilometres from land, many birds were largely dependent on human activities. It was a salutary lesson that the influence of humanity is all-pervasive.

On most trips offshore I was the only ornithologist on board the ship. It was usually too expensive to commission vessels specifically to survey seabirds, so the Seabirds at Sea team posted lone observers on ships that were offshore for other reasons. We used a mixture of fisheries research vessels, passenger ferries and even Royal Navy fisheries patrol vessels. On one occasion the navy ship I was working from was diverted from its normal task of checking to see if fishing boats were operating legally, to something rather more out of the ordinary. A helicopter landed on deck and a team of heavily armed uniforms spilled from its side, before I was obliged to jump aboard and head back to shore – it would not have been appropriate for a civilian to witness whatever may have been about to happen.

On days when there was exciting wildlife on view, being the only interested observer brought a strange mixture of feelings. On the one hand it was a privilege to be seeing things that were well out of reach to land-based observers. Watching huge concentrations of seabirds around fishing boats southwest of the Isles of Scilly, tens of kilometres from land, was a rare opportunity indeed. But, at the same time, it was frustrating not to be able to share the experience or discuss observations with like-minded individuals.

A few years ago Hazel and I went on a whale-watching trip out of Victoria on Vancouver Island, off the west coast of Canada. As the boat homed in on the local resident pod of Orcas, we found ourselves sharing the experience with not only the forty people on our boat, but also at least thirty other boatloads of whale watchers. I couldn't help but feel this devalued the experience. It wasn't because the animals were inconvenienced in any way; there are strict rules to ensure that boats keep a safe distance. But the experience emphasised just how much humans dominate the planet. Here we were bobbing around on a boat with perhaps twenty Orcas and as many as 500 people sharing the same small area of sea.

Over the years, lone observation of wildlife has become a recurring theme. I'm drawn to places where I am the only person present and the wildlife takes centre stage. Even our choices of house over the years have been influenced by their isolation and a surrounding countryside little visited by other people. It's not easy to explain the appeal, or even fully understand it, but when I try to do so, the experience with those Orcas often comes to mind. In my Seabirds at Sea days, I was sometimes the only person watching wildlife across thousands of square kilometres of sea. Then, of course, I missed the company of fellow enthusiasts. It seems we are never happy.

WESTERN ISLES REFUGE

We once spent ten days in a cottage on a wild and rugged peninsula on Skye in northwest Scotland. Leaving the Fens far behind us, we swapped our island of trees in the arable prairies for a real island and a landscape that could hardly be more different. On a previous visit, many years earlier, a short but pleasant boat trip had been required to complete the journey. But now, rather than having to wait in a line of cars for the ferry, the transition from mainland to island was completed in less than a minute using the road bridge. These days, if you're not paying attention, you can easily miss the fact that you've arrived on Skye. I'm sure the people who live in the area appreciate the bridge, and it seems churlish to think that it's a bit of a shame it was built. I can imagine trying to argue the point with local people. The islanders patiently explaining how much time it saves and how it has made it easier and cheaper to bring in supplies; me mumbling something about how a little bit of the island's 'magic' has been lost, whatever that might mean. Actually, after an energy-sapping drive of twelve hours, there was a part of me (quite a big part) that was glad of the bridge and its time-saving benefits.

We decided to visit Skye in mid-January for a number of reasons. First and foremost we were seeking peace, quiet and, for want of a better word, remoteness. I was keen to finish a writing project and thought it would be easier with ten days free from the usual distractions of life back home. We chose as isolated a cottage as we could find and, in contrast to our usual family holidays, the lack of wi-fi was a welcome bonus. The next house was more than a kilometre away down a single-track road that saw hardly any traffic. Staying in such a remote place reminded me of something my mother has always said about the perils of isolation. She feels uncomfortable staying anywhere that is far enough from the rest of humanity that help could not be summoned (should it be required) through shouting or screaming. Despite the shared DNA I feel the exact opposite, preferring places sufficiently remote that the shouts and screams (and music and lawn mowers) of others cannot be heard.

We could probably have found somewhere equally remote without spending quite so long in the car, but I have a special affection for the Western Isles and welcomed the chance of reconnecting with wildlife that is not so easily found further south. Although the long journey was not exactly enjoyable, the time taken to get there played its part in achieving the desired sense of disconnection from normal life. A few hours in a plane could have taken us much further from home but would not have had the same effect as the twelve-hour journey by road. The more rapidly and painlessly a wild, remote place can be reached, the less wild and remote it feels, and something of its specialness is lost. In a nutshell, that's my feeling about the road bridge. The fact that it makes things easier is the very thing that diminishes the place (just a little bit) as a refuge for visitors seeking 'wildness', if not for the majority of residents.

Another reason for heading north was to get a feel for life there at the least promising time of year in terms of weather conditions and hours of daylight. Hazel and I have talked about living somewhere like this in future, and while I'd have no problems with this in summer, I wondered whether the sustained grey and gloom of midwinter might take its toll. I once lived in Aberdeen for two years and can't say I found the winters there to be a significant issue, though that was a long time ago when youth was on my side. Hazel has never stayed anywhere so far north in winter. Taking into account family commitments leading up to Christmas and the New Year, arriving in the second week in January was as close as we could get to the shortest day of the year and, we thought, the best chance of experiencing the worst that winter could throw at us.

As it happened, we had a mixed bag of weather with severe gales, rain, sleet, hail, snow and even lightning during our ten days. It was exceptionally cold for the far west coast, and after several nights of sub-zero temperatures the freshwater lochs were frozen and exposed rocks covered with an invisible, and potentially lethal, glaze of ice. Rounded cushions of green and red-tinged *Sphagnum* moss crunched rather than squelched underfoot. There were a few days when, admittedly, we did feel rather battered by the relentlessly strong wind, and were driven back indoors by sleet and snow, flung horizontally into our faces. One morning, after overnight gales, we were alarmed to find rubbish from the outside bin strewn all around the garden, lodged in every available recess and blocking most of the holes used by the garden's burgeoning Rabbit population. The bin itself had to be retrieved from the rocky shore 100 metres away. We also had several days of mainly calm and sunny conditions, and we enjoyed them all the more knowing they wouldn't last. Overall, the varied conditions were refreshing and invigorating rather than in any way dispiriting.

Surprisingly, the amount of daylight was not a major issue either. Light levels changed more slowly than further south. The daily descent into darkness in late afternoon was noticeably gradual, wholly in keeping with the pace of life in general. Sunset was just after 4.00 p.m. but, on a clear day, a full hour later it was still possible to make out the faint orange and pink glow from buoys marking the lobster-pots out in the loch. It felt like we were being eased, as painlessly as possible, into the long dark winter night. The extension of the early-morning and late-afternoon transitions from night to day and back again lengthened the two periods that are best for watching wildlife and for seeing the scenery at its finest.

The Western Isles in midwinter is not the place to come to amass a huge holiday list of wildlife, though there are some exciting and enigmatic species to enjoy. Within walking distance of the cottage we saw numerous White-tailed Eagles, an adult Golden Eagle, an Otter working its way along the shore in the middle of the day, and some remarkably confiding Common Seals that followed us back and forth along the deserted beach, at times just a few metres away. They were perhaps mainly interested in our dog, and they bobbed up and down like periscopes, straining for a better view. Every so often they would all throw themselves underwater in apparent alarm with a rapid-fire series of sharp 'slaps'. Then, before long, curiosity would get the better of them and they'd re-emerge to continue their wide-eyed staring.

On one of the calmest days I watched a group of Harbour Porpoises offshore, surfacing in that unique way they have – offering just the briefest glimpse of a dark back and diminutive dorsal fin. They are the plodders of the cetacean world, though delightful nonetheless. There were also the expected Great Northern and Red-throated Divers, excitable groups of Red-breasted Mergansers and a handful of Black Guillemots along the wildest stretches of coast. On the beach nearest to the house we came across a first-year Glaucous Gull standing with a small group of Herring and Great Black-backed Gulls – its 'dipped-in-ink' bill-tip was almost invisible against the dark backdrop of rocks, but the rest of the bird shone out brightly like an Arctic beacon.

Yet, on one two-hour walk across expansive open moorland, I saw just four Red Deer, a couple of Wrens (of course) and a single Woodcock, flying up a few paces ahead of me. I would expect to see a far greater diversity of wildlife back at home, though I could certainly not hope to replicate the feeling of isolation and remoteness, or the spectacular and invigorating wild scenery.

Gavin Maxwell wrote *Ring of Bright Water* not too far from where we were staying, on the mainland just across the water from Skye. This classic book describes Maxwell's experiences living alongside the wildlife at his remote cottage on the west coast of the Highlands and, in particular, his tame otters.* I read it for the first time before we travelled and was struck particularly

---

* Maxwell, G. (1960) *Ring of Bright Water*. Longman, London. I was surprised to learn that the otters were not the native species but imported animals of two different kinds from the Middle East and Africa.

by his thoughts on first arriving at the place that was to be his home, on and off, for ten years:

> In the British Isles it is a strange sensation to lie down to sleep knowing that there is no human being within a mile and a half in any direction . . . But to be quite alone where there are no other human beings is sharply exhilarating; it is as though some pressure had suddenly been lifted, allowing an intense awareness of one's surroundings, a sharpening of the senses, and an intimate recognition of the teeming sub-human life around one.

I'd certainly agree with these sentiments; though, for me, the real sharpening of the senses comes from walking in remote landscapes rather than lying down to sleep within the confines and security of four walls. It is indeed an exhilarating experience. In the part of Skye we visited, mobile reception was virtually non-existent. When you are alone, exploring rugged sea-cliffs on a freezing winter afternoon with the light fading and several kilometres of steep, undulating terrain between you and the nearest building, even a minor accident could have serious consequences. Something as trivial as a sprained ankle would make it very difficult to reach safety and warmth, or the nearest human able to provide assistance. That knowledge both heightens the senses and makes the more typical worries of everyday life fade to insignificance. Connection with the landscape and awareness of surroundings becomes more real and intense, out of necessity. Lose concentration here and you could end up as food for eagles.

As on previous occasions when spending time in remote, wild, locations, it made me wonder why I so readily submit to the rigours of normal life, far removed from a meaningful connection with the natural world. Why do I put up with the higher levels of pressure and the dulling of the senses that come as an inevitable part of spending so much time jammed together with other people on clogged roads and in packed urban centres? To judge by the comments in the cottage's visitor book, others shared these sentiments. There were long messages delighting in sightings of Otters, White-tailed Eagles and other wildlife, as well as frequent references to the dramatic wild landscape and its restorative effects. I noticed that many of the comments emphasised the problems of normal life back home as much as the delights of being able to avoid it for a short time: 'a welcome rest-bite from city life', 'wonderful to be able to find some peace and quiet *for a change*' and 'a marvellous escape from the rat-race' were typical examples.

Hazel, it has to be said, was rather less enamoured with the isolation, the rugged, empty landscapes and the nagging wind. She enjoyed the wildlife and the scenery but, after ten days, she was more than ready to get back to familiar surroundings and the routine of normal life. In terms of a potential future house move, we had plenty to talk about during the long trek back through the snow-covered Highlands, and on the increasingly busy roads heading south through England.

A CHANGE OF SCENE

After twenty-five years working for Natural England and living in the flatlands of Cambridgeshire I finally decided I'd had enough of both. I was slow to realise it, but the job and the local landscape had both been wearing me down for some time. I solved the job problem by taking early retirement. And once free from work, Hazel and I started to think about moving away from Cambridgeshire.

It's often pointed out that the United Kingdom is one of the most densely populated countries on the planet, a place where the natural world is more effectively constrained and shackled by humanity than almost anywhere else. Within the UK, England supports the highest density of people and the most intensive land management. And within England, the fenland country of Lincolnshire and Cambridgeshire represents perhaps our greatest achievement in subverting the natural world to our own ends. A huge area of once impenetrable floodplain and marshland, teeming with wildlife, now serves as some of the most productive and intensively managed arable farmland in Europe. Despite a lifelong passion for wildlife and remote places, I'd managed to spend twenty-five years of my life living here, surrounded by intensification, through a combination of circumstances and apathy. We had made the best of what the Fens had to offer, but it was time for a change.

We were looking for a contrast with the arable-dominated landscapes of the east, and the Southwest Peninsula offered one, without taking us too far away from friends and family. We rented a house on a dairy farm in sparsely populated mid-Devon, halfway between Exmoor and Dartmoor. To some extent we swapped intensive arable farming for intensively farmed dairy cows, sheep and chickens. The farmer we rent the house from has 400 cows that spend their lives inside a huge shed, fitted out with the latest high-tech equipment. The cows milk themselves using robots, and their tags send a message to his mobile to alert him to any problems. From the upstairs windows of the house we can see the low, brooding sheds of an intensive chicken farm across the valley. A mass of tiny white dots spill out from its flanks each morning, littering the surrounding field to such an extent that you wonder how they could possibly all fit back inside.

But amid the intensification are pockets of interesting wildlife habitat. Within a few hundred metres of the house there are overgrown hedgerows, small deciduous woods, old meadows and boggy, rush-infested, flower-rich fields. In contrast to the Fens, forgotten corners rich in wildlife are part of the normal landscape, rather than restricted solely to isolated nature reserves.

The landscape is big enough and sparsely populated enough to support wild animals that require space and seclusion. In fact, it supports our largest land mammal in numbers that came as a revelation. I'm used to seeing Muntjac in ones and twos, and Roe Deer in small groups. But the local Red Deer appear in their dozens, and dominate a scene as effectively as a field full of cows.

They can be unpredictable, going missing from the local fields for weeks at a time. Then, suddenly, they are back again, thirty or more, filling a field that, one glance ago, had been empty. They are so effective at utilising the undulating landscape, the small pockets of woodland and the dense, overgrown hedge-lines, that they seem able to materialise out of the ether – an effect all the more powerful on days with a low mist to blur the sightlines.

During the protracted autumn rut we often hear the stags roaring at night. Once, at the peak of the rut, I almost stumbled into a mature stag as I was about to step out from the edge of a wood. There he was, no more than thirty metres away in the adjacent field, breath steaming up into the cool October air. For a moment he stood his ground, glaring with an intensity that pushed me backwards a few steps and had me checking the nearest trees for footholds. Then he stomped slowly away, throwing a face-saving snort in my direction as he turned – a snort of derision if ever there was one.

A few months later, on New Year's Day, I came across a dead stag in the middle of a woodland stream, already starting to show signs of decomposition. I edged closer to the stream, trying to ignore the stench, and did a double take. There were four antlers, not two. Although one body was partly hidden in the water, I was looking at two dead stags. More slowly than I'm keen to admit, it dawned on me what had happened. These were rutting stags whose antlers had become locked together in combat. Unable to separate themselves and weakened by the fight, they ended up at the base of the slope in the stream at the valley bottom. Here they succumbed, over who knows how many days, with death the only possible outcome. I went back the next day with a handsaw and removed the antlers, a cloud of hot bone dust from the saw mixing with the smell of putrefying flesh. We now have a deer-antler coat rack in the hall, and I think back to that day every time I take my jacket down.

The Red Deer add a wild element to the local area because of their size and numbers, but also because of their behaviour. They are able to utilise the whole landscape because it is still sufficiently well connected and subject to minimal human disturbance. I can spend hours walking through the woods and fields and see no-one. Any farmer I come across out in the fields is usually ensconced within the cab of a tractor, which for me means less chance of a telling-off for wandering across private farmland and, for the deer, less perceived danger. Whenever I encounter herds of deer I try to avoid disturbing them by watching from a distance and altering my route to move around them. But occasionally I have blundered too close by mistake and their response reaffirms their wildness. Eyes bulge with fear and then, if not reassured that all is well, thundering hooves replace the silence.

Living in this new, unfamiliar place, I've made a conscious effort to try to reconnect with nature. I had promised myself this. Having worked for so long at Natural England, there was a reasonable payoff on leaving – enough to cover at least two years of not working. I wanted to use that time to get over the feelings of disillusionment that had come to dominate my thoughts about nature conservation. I wanted to renew the bond with nature that, until recently, had always been such a big part of my life but I felt had been slipping away. For the first time in years I spent long hours out in the countryside almost every day. Sometimes I had the company of Teazel, our errant, wildlife-unfriendly

Cocker Spaniel, but often I was alone. I would either walk from the house or drive a few kilometres, park up, and walk out to explore somewhere a little less familiar. This wouldn't have worked very well in the flatlands of the Cambridgeshire Fens, but in mid-Devon it was time well spent.

To some extent, it has had the effect I was hoping for. I have felt the benefits of welcoming nature back into my life, gradually tuning in to the daily and seasonal rhythms of the area in a way that is only possible if you have the time to visit the same places day after day. The Red Deer are regular companions, but there is plenty of other wildlife. And I've caught up with a few creatures that had eluded me my entire life, satisfying my latent birder's instinct for 'ticks'. There are Small Pearl-bordered Fritillaries along Bracken-covered slopes and Marsh Fritillaries in the damper hollows where their food-plant, Devil's-bit Scabious, grows. Last autumn I found the highly esteemed edible Chanterelle and Cep fungi for the first time, bringing a few home for lunch. I even persuaded Hazel to eat them, though only after I'd survived for a few days after the first meal.

I finally saw my first (and second) Harvest Mouse. I'd noticed their nests of tightly woven grass stems – barely bigger than a squash ball – tucked away in tussocks of Purple Moor-grass in the local fields. Knowing they were in the area, I started to set live-catch small mammal traps in the garden, hoping my laid-back mowing regime would pay dividends. After several nights with no more than a few hyperactive Wood Mice and the occasional Field Vole, I lifted a trap that felt unpromisingly weightless. Expecting nothing, I emptied the contents – and amongst the straw bedding and seeds I was amazed to see not one but two Harvest Mice spill out into the bucket. Being such nimble and lightweight animals, the first had failed to spring the trap and the second had followed it in, trapping them both. Perhaps they were foraging as a team?

A hand offered into the bucket revealed the strong climbing instinct that allows Harvest Mice to live out their lives amongst the fragile grass stems. One scaled my arm before I could think to stop it. Most animals are programmed to run away or dive for cover when they feel threatened. The Wood Mice I caught bounded off at lightning speed, often leaping clear of the bucket for their first trick. The Field Voles tried to nose their way into the bucket's hard plastic bottom, and when placed back into the grass I understood why. They dived down into the thatch of dead grass, dissolving into the vegetation away from threatening eyes and claws. In contrast, the response of a Harvest Mouse to a novel situation is to run 'up'. No doubt they feel safer from predators at the tops of grass stems. Anything heavier than a Harvest Mouse would cause the vegetation to fold down to the ground and end any pursuit of prey.

Another animal I am delighted to see regularly is the majestic Goshawk. This isn't an entirely new species, but Goshawks are notoriously elusive and my previous encounters had been mostly distant specks in the sky or fleeting glimpses of blurred shapes weaving through the trees. Here, they are sufficiently common in the local countryside that I see them every few days. I hear their sharp, scolding calls in the spring if I inadvertently walk too close to a nest site.

That's how I came across a pair nesting in the wood closest to our house. They can be watched from the windows when they are above the canopy, spiralling in circles over the trees, diving malevolently at passing Buzzards, or heading out across the fields to hunt, often leaving a trail of irate corvids in their wake. Measuring out a straight line on the map revealed that the nest is just 400 metres from the edge of our garden. Raised voices around the patio chairs are surely audible to the adults, and I try to visualise the bird on its nest, turning one of its piercing orange eyes accusingly in our direction. For much of the year, unless you keep a careful eye out for them, they are easy to overlook, even though they are breeding so close by. But in late summer, when the young leave the nest, their distinctive whistling cries ring out across the valley as they try to elicit food from their overworked parents.

These new connections with wildlife are exactly what I needed. My relationship with the natural world had been sorely tested at times in the intensively managed farmland of eastern England where I'd spent so many years. Here in mid-Devon, in a place with more wild spaces and more variation in the landscape, my relationship with nature has been rekindled, and I feel all the more human for that.

WESTERN ISLES REVISITED

Another opportunity to visit the Hebrides presented itself in the autumn of 2018. The trip was part of a writing project involving a long spell of immersion in nature and detachment from the wider connections of humanity. I'd already chosen a small Hebridean island that I had never visited before as a potential location for a long-term stay, aided by implausible online images of sun-drenched white-sand beaches, and idyllic rolling moorland. The obvious next step, before launching headlong into the full trip, was a dose of realism. I needed to go there for a short break in order to get a feel for the place at first hand. An autumn 'recce' was suggested and (with the promise of sun-drenched beaches) Hazel gladly agreed. We organised two weeks in the remotest of the cottages rented out by the island's main estate, and headed north on a not-so-sun-drenched late September day.

Despite the rigours of the long drive that lay ahead, my mood started to lift as we headed north through increasingly unfamiliar territory. Once past the busy sections of the M6 in the urban north-west of England, the landscape opened out and the traffic died away. The distant sharp peaks of the Lake District slid by on one side and the low hills of the Yorkshire Dales offered a contrast on the other. There was one final battle to come, but once Glasgow had been safely negotiated, the traffic thinned again, this time for good. The narrow main road winding its way north along the shores of Loch Lomond was littered with sodden leaves and debris from Storm Ali, which had blown through earlier in the day. My daughter was delighted to hear that a storm had been named after her, and was appropriately contrite when told it had slowed our progress a little.

Then came the CalMac ferry from Oban, the main urban centre and port on the west coast of the Highlands. Without fail, I spend my time on a boat up on deck looking out over the sea. Perhaps it's partly down to a susceptibility to seasickness when confined inside a moving ship, but mainly it's a hangover from the time I spent working for the Seabirds at Sea team. To help derive estimates of seabird numbers we learnt to visualise a transect, 200 metres wide, on one side of the ship. By recording all birds using that transect the figures could be multiplied up to estimate the overall numbers of birds using each area. All these years later, my brain is still drawn towards the same approach, projecting an imaginary line across the ocean and trying not to miss anything on my side of it.

The seabirds on this journey were all routine fare for the time of year but welcome nonetheless. Despite my days recording seabirds I've spent most of my life well inland in the southern half of England. Whole years can slip by without seeing common seabirds such as Guillemots, Razorbills and Kittiwakes. There were small groups of all three as we headed west away from the mainland. The auks sitting on the sea closest to the boat performed their usual trick as we approached them, wings becoming flippers as they threw themselves underwater and disappeared – trying to evade detection in my imaginary transect. I was delighted to

see a few juvenile Kittiwakes with their distinctive black zigzag
lines on the upper wings. This, to my mind, is our most subtly
graceful and elegant seabird, the adults with their delicate grey
and white wings and contrasting jet-black tips. It's a bird that
has struggled badly in recent years due to declining stocks of
sandeels, its staple food in the breeding season, most likely caused
by a combination of overfishing and warming seas. A few pairs,
at least, had managed to find enough food to rear their young.
A brief, if unexpected, reminder of home came in the form of
some distant dull-brown dots on the remote southern shores of
Mull a few kilometres to the north as we passed by. They could
only have been Red Deer, and they helped to highlight the vast
scale of the landscape around them – our largest land mammal
reduced to tiny specks, dwarfed by the rocks and moorland all
around them. On the other side of the ship were the islands of
Scarba and Jura, and the menacing waters of the Gulf of
Corryvreckan between them. The tidal races and whirlpools here
are notorious, and almost accounted for George Orwell in 1947
during a family boating trip, potentially depriving the world of
Nineteen Eighty-Four, which had still to be finished.

After two and a half hours the ferry slowed and performed a
series of unlikely juddering contortions, easing alongside a pier
that, to the untrained eye, seemed inadequate for its job. Most
people stayed in their seats, awaiting the onward journey to Islay,
but we made our way down to the vehicle deck and joined a
handful of other people heading onto one of the smaller and
more sparsely populated islands of the Inner Hebrides.

If you read anything about the island of Colonsay you won't go far before you come across a reference to 'the Scottish Highlands and Islands in miniature'. A cursory assessment from the deck of the ferry, followed by a twenty-minute drive around the island's only single-track loop road, showed us why it had earned the epithet. Colonsay is about twelve kilometres long and five wide, on average, and yet it has a little of almost every broad habitat the Highlands has to offer. Inland, it is dominated by low, rocky hills and open moorland; an intimate patchwork of dry heathland and treacherous waterlogged bogs, as I later discovered when venturing out on foot. The highest point is 143 metres, very much a mini-mountain in Scottish terms, yet more than enough to get the blood pumping and provide a spectacular view over the island and its surroundings. Much of the coastline is made up of low, wild rocky shore but there are also sections of sheer cliffs, swarming with seabirds in the breeding season, as well as contrasting long, wide sandy beaches. There are extensive dunes and saltmarshes, and on the strand between Colonsay and its smaller neighbour Oronsay, to the south, an expanse of wader-friendly mudflats. There is also an area of planted woodland around the big house of the island's main estate – a mix of conifers and broadleaves, including some impressively large trees.

Natural deciduous woodland is a habitat that would once have dominated the Highlands. Swathes of impenetrable woods and scrub would have greeted early human visitors to the region. After centuries of felling, burning, and grazing by livestock and deer, it has largely disappeared, but even here, Colonsay comes good. There is a sizeable wood of mixed native trees above the eastern shoreline that has somehow survived, offering a magical contrast with the more typical, but less natural, open landscape across the rest of the island.

For a small island, Colonsay presents huge contrasts over relatively small distances in other aspects as well as habitats. The west-facing coast is exposed to the vastness of the open ocean and the prevailing westerly wind. Even on a calm day the swell rolls in relentlessly, each wave sending up white plumes of spray as it meets immovable rock, or plunging down onto the beach as it finally expires. The eastern side is more protected and sheltered. On a calm day the sea on this side of the island looks almost completely flat. Point a telescope out to sea on the east coast, even on a breezy day, and you may notice groups of Eider bobbing offshore and perhaps pick out mergansers, or divers of any of our three common species. Try the same thing, on the same day, on the west coast and even if you can hold the telescope steady on its tripod, the birds will be all but impossible to see. No doubt they are there, but they are hidden away among the troughs and peaks of the waves, and the wind-thrown white-caps.

There is another contrast too. While nowhere on Colonsay could be described as busy with people, if you visit the largest of the sandy beaches at Kiloran or the strand between Colonsay and Oronsay, which is walkable at low tide, you are likely to have at least some company as you head off for your stroll. But walk away from the road inland, or set out across the moorland to the coastline away from roads and paths, and you will soon be walking in a remote, wild landscape with few signs of humanity and almost no prospect of seeing another soul. That sort of experience is increasingly hard to find in Britain, particularly in areas rich in wildlife.

We found our cottage, tucked away in a fold of land at the end of a long track across rough, sheep-grazed moorland. It was in the southeast of the island, looking out over the sea and across the sound to the remote, uninhabited, western coastline of Jura. A welcoming 'ring-tail' Hen Harrier cruised past a few hundred metres away not long after we arrived, hugging the contours, constantly adjusting and readjusting its flight path as it investigated potential prey. There were no other houses visible – just moorland, a low rocky coastline, and the sea beyond. I could see myself spending time in a place like this.

The next day, we came across a freshly dead sheep not far from the house, interrupting the feeding aspirations of a young Great Black-backed Gull and two Hooded Crows as we approached. It was so fresh, I half-expected it to struggle to its feet, but the eyes were already bloodied and hollowed out, and I guessed it had been dead for a few hours at least. I wondered whether I might be able to track the progress of a dead sheep over several months if I returned for a longer stay, to find out just how valuable it would be as a food source. How long would it take before the whole animal disappeared into the food chain? How many different species would it support through the lean winter months? I could watch from a distance for perhaps an hour every day, hoping that one of the island's eagles might put in an appearance.

After a few days of getting to know Colonsay, with lots of short drives and walks to the most accessible places, I thought it was time to venture out into one of the more remote and wilder parts of the island. A look at the Ordnance Survey map drew me to the far northeastern corner, away from roads and tracks, and lacking even footpaths. It included the remote area of native woodland I'd seen from the ferry, flanked by several square kilometres of uninhabited, empty moorland on three sides, and a long stretch of low rocky coastline on the other. I parked in the dunes above Kiloran Bay early in the day and headed east, across the moor, towards the opposite coast.

It was tough going in places. The wetter areas of bog threatened to overwhelm my walking boots, and I started to scan further ahead, looking out for vegetation that thrives in waterlogged ground. It was too late in the season for the normally reliable cottongrasses, so the fiery, orange flower-spikes of Bog Asphodel were the most helpful indicators. I avoided these, despite their aesthetic appeal, and headed instead for areas covered with Bracken or purple-flowering heathers, plants that favour drier ground. From a high vantage point I could use binoculars to plot a likely route ahead for a few hundred metres at a time. I kept my feet dry but the Bracken and heather came with their own problems. In the absence of heavy grazing by livestock, both plants were sometimes well above head height – perhaps the tallest heather I had ever seen. At times I was walking under the vegetation rather than through it, pushing between the stiff stems and, on several occasions, finding that my rucksack had become ensnared in a tangled mesh of branches.

After about an hour I reached the edge of the woodland, sloping away to the shore below me, and descended into an enchanted world beneath the canopy. The trees weren't tall but

the thick lower branches were twisted and contorted in all directions away from their trunks, some no more than a few
centimetres above the ground. They were all familiar species –
oaks and birches dominated, but Rowan, Ash and Hazel were
also present. And yet the shapes and the colours lent the wood
an unfamiliar feel. Mosses and ferns grew profusely from the
branches, and lichens of varying shades and textures patterned
the bark. Beneath the trees was more head-high Bracken, the
leaves blending greens, browns and yellows as they began their
decay towards winter. The wood felt slightly surreal, almost wrong
for the place. And yet if anything was wrong, or at least less
natural, it was the vast open area beyond the woodland edge.
Adding to the surreal experience were the calls of Curlew and
Oystercatcher, filtering up through the trees from the shoreline
below. There was also a mournful, almost human, wailing that I
couldn't place, which had me turning in all directions trying to
pinpoint it. It was another two hours before I worked out where
it was coming from.

The Hazel trees were covered with ripe nuts, something that
the introduced Grey Squirrels rarely allow to happen in the
woods I'm more familiar with. I was searching for a stone to
crack open a few of them, rather than risk my teeth, when it
slowly dawned on me that I was being watched. I was about to
experience something that has happened to me only a handful
of times before in Britain. A lone Great Tit started things
off, landing in the nearest birch and firing a gentle burst of
staccato, machine-gun chattering in my direction. It was a call to
arms, quickly answered by four more Great Tits and then other
species too, including Chaffinches, Goldcrests, Long-tailed Tits

and Blue Tits, all edging closer to me, intently focused on my presence. Boldest of all was a tiny Coal Tit. It moved gradually further out towards me in the branches of the birch tree, ending up so close that I thought about reaching out a hand to see if it would hop on.

It's a strange, almost overpowering, feeling to be the subject of such intense curiosity from a whole community of wild birds, and when it has happened before it has been, as here, in the wildest and remotest of places. These birds were genuinely bemused to see a creature that was unfamiliar to them and had suddenly, unexpectedly, appeared in their wood. The location made it easy to believe that many of them, especially those reared this summer, had never seen a person before and were interested to watch one for a while to see what it would do next. No doubt birds across the land reacted in much the same way to the first humans to enter their world many thousands of years ago, little suspecting the huge changes they would bring with them. About half an hour later I encountered what I took to be the same flock a little lower down the slope, and this time I was rudely ignored. They were not going to waste valuable feeding time again, having already made their assessment.

Away from the mixed bird flock the woods were largely silent. There were a few rushed snatches of song from unseen Wrens, almost apologetic in their brevity and lack of spring vigour. The only other bird noise was made by Robins, perhaps our most underappreciated songster. Its voice has a melancholy beauty that no other bird can match. In spring it is often drowned out by the louder, brasher songs that demand our attention. But in autumn its soft outpourings can be savoured, each one trailing gently away into the silence that follows, leaving you waiting in anticipation for the next instalment.

Down on the shore, away from the trees, the feel of the place was very different. The magic of the woodland on the slopes above was closed off from view by a shielding canopy of leaves, and the wood itself was dwarfed by the open moorland surrounding it. I walked out towards the end of a narrow peninsula and noticed two Feral Goats, moving ahead of me through the dense heather. I'd read about Colonsay's famous wild goats, including the unlikely assertion that they first arrived when a ship from the Spanish Armada was wrecked on the island's rocks. They had certainly been here for a long time, and their presence is not good news for the long-term future of the woodland. Goats are a notoriously destructive non-native species and have devastated the natural vegetation of islands all around the world.

As I reached the edge of the rocks I realised that the two animals had become separated as they tried to avoid me. An adult was further along the shore about fifty metres away, looking anxiously back towards a small, sandy-coloured kid just a short distance ahead of me. Inadvertently, I'd been blocking its escape route, leaving it staring out to sea wondering what to do next. I moved as far to one side as was possible on the narrow spit of rocks, but it was too late. The kid hesitated for a few seconds and then launched itself into the air, landing on a low rocky island on the far side of a narrow channel of water. I worried that as the tide came in it might be cut off as the channel widened. Destructive non-native or not, I felt compelled to do something, and the only real option was to follow it onto the island and then try to persuade it to make the leap back to land.

I'm glad there was no-one around to watch my ungainly rescue attempt, though, at the same time, I was conscious that if I twisted an ankle, or worse, there was no help nearby, and no mobile phone signal. I crash-landed onto the island and then picked my way carefully around it, placing my boots onto barnacle-encrusted rocks where the footing was secure, and avoiding the layers of wet, slippery kelp and wrack in between. I edged my way clockwise around the island, pushing the frightened kid ahead of me in the same direction. Once back facing the mainland it needed no second invitation, leaping across and somehow sticking like glue to the rocks on the far side, despite the slope and the uneven surface. I mirrored its jump, if not its dexterity and sure-footedness, and managed to make it back to shore unscathed.

There were more goats as I walked north along the coast, up to a dozen at a time, with almost the same number of variations of coat colour and pattern. I found one of the handsome back-curving horns washed up on the beach and was impressed by its strength for something so light in the hand. It was reinforced with raised rings, rough to the touch, all along its length, as well as a thickened leading edge. Attached to a goat, there was no doubting it would make a formidable weapon.

I had regular company from another mammal over the next few hours, and the mystery of the unearthly wailing was finally resolved. Away from the woods and having heard the cries again, I'd already guessed the identity – and a bright white dot on the rocks ahead provided confirmation. Grey Seals breed in the autumn, often choosing rocky coastlines and sea-caves to give birth, in places where disturbance is minimal. The pup almost glowed against the black rocks and dark brown seaweed. I wondered why evolution hadn't equipped it to blend into the background. Perhaps the risk of a mother losing track of its offspring on the rocks is greater than any threat of predation, or perhaps it's a hangover from colder times when pups would have been born on ice and snow. I was keen not to disturb it, but without retracing my steps I had no choice but to pass by only about ten metres away, the low cliffs above the beach being too treacherous to climb. I needn't have worried. The pup was well grown, over a metre long, with its head half-hidden behind a boulder and its body heaving rhythmically up and down. It lacked the good grace even to acknowledge my presence as I walked by.

There were more pups further on, and I found a place where I could watch from a safe distance. Each pup was attended by a female, either hauled out on the edge of the rocks or swimming in the sea just offshore. There were also male seals along the shoreline, their huge bulk and long roman noses clearly setting them apart from the more refined females. The males regularly visited the females looking for mating opportunities, resulting in bouts of frenzied interactions that involved much twisting, rolling and splashing in the water. It was difficult to work out whether the females were willing participants in these coupling rituals or were trying to repel unwanted advances. The pups, in contrast, were unambiguous in their response, their wailing cries coinciding with the activity just offshore. They must have been aware of the commotion in the water and preferred to have their mother's attention all to themselves. At one point two large males came together in the water and started to fight. They disappeared beneath the surface only to reappear, the mouth of one gaping open, teeth bearing down onto the neck of the other as, once more, they slid beneath the waves.

A few days later I went back to the northeast of the island, this time with my fishing rod, threading it through the tall Bracken stems as I walked, or even hoisting it over my head above the dense canopy of fronds. I'd not managed to find anywhere else on Colonsay with deep water within easy reach of the rocks, but here conditions seemed perfect.

Sea fishing is one of the most complete and fulfilling ways of spending time in nature. There is the solitude (at least on this occasion), with no-one else for miles around. There is the need to read the landscape and the tide in order to find a decent spot to fish from. And there is the mix of both terrestrial and marine wildlife, depending on which way you turn your head as you stand at the interface between the two. More than that, you are getting your hands dirty and directly interacting with wildlife rather than simply watching it go by. There is, hopefully, the handling of the fish, its rapid despatch and the knowledge that, later, you will eat what you have caught. That, in itself, plays to one of our most basic instincts. In a rare departure from the norm, it is a pastime unencumbered by the restrictions of officialdom. No permissions, permits or licences are required. It is free and open to everyone. It's not much fun for the fish, of course, but there is the consolation that each one is caught in the most sustainable way possible, harming nothing else in the process.

I fished using a spinner – a heavy, shiny piece of metal, repeatedly cast out and reeled back in to mimic a small bait fish. It requires less patience than casting out a stationary bait and waiting, and it burns more calories. Offshore there were a few Shags, a distant Great Northern Diver, a scattering of Eiders and a Black Guillemot that had already lost its dapper black-and-white plumage from the summer, sporting an untidier, almost dishevelled, mottled-all-over effect. A Shag came closer in to the rocks as it fished, each dive launched with a refined leap forward into the water. The larger Cormorant lacks this graceful prelude, flopping inelegantly underwater without the jump. In areas where both species occur, as here around Colonsay, the difference in diving technique can be a helpful way to distinguish between the two. As a soundtrack there was silence, the gentle lap of water against rock, or the mournful, haunting duet between Curlews and a seal pup missing its mother.

After a few minutes the Shag came within my casting range and so I paused from fishing, wary after an experience the previous summer in Sutherland. On that occasion a lone Guillemot was fishing in the water nearby. I didn't think anything of it, and when I felt a hard rattle and tug on the rod I simply assumed that I'd hooked another Mackerel. Then the line went slack and up to the surface bobbed the Guillemot, looking somewhat shaken as it ruffled its feathers back into place. It had been fooled in the same way as the Mackerel I'd already caught and was lucky to have avoided the hooks. With the benefit of hindsight, I suppose the incident was unsurprising. If a fish thinks a piece of metal is another fish, then why wouldn't a fish-eating bird make the same mistake?

There were no Mackerel here after an hour of fishing, and I wondered if, in early October, it was already a little late in the season, and they had retreated further offshore for the winter. I'd reached the stage where every new cast was to be the last one. Forty minutes later, it finally paid off.

The Mackerel is a fish sent from heaven. Everything about it brings joy. I find it reassuring that despite all the damage caused by overfishing, if you cast your line into deep water anywhere along the west coast of Britain in summer, you will likely catch them. They roam the seas restlessly in packs, like miniature tuna, constantly on the move, snapping at anything that resembles food. Even a bare hook can sometimes catch one if the glint of thin, polished metal draws its eye. Strings of feathers (each hiding a hook) take advantage of the pack mentality. The first fish snaps at its 'prey', and the others see this and move in, looking to take advantage of a feeding opportunity. They cannot afford a more considered approach – they would lose their meal to the next fish.

Mackerel are stunningly beautiful, with a streamlined, torpedo-like shape and a series of short, triangular 'go-faster' finlets towards the tail. They are delicately patterned with dark wavy stripes that cut across an iridescent green-blue background on the upper surface, onto the silvery flanks below. These stripes, apparently, are used as visual markers by the fish to help keep the school together. On a bright day you know you've caught a Mackerel when it is still several feet underwater as the sun lights up the gaps between the stripes, and the whole fish flickers. This is a fish that you must catch for yourself if you want to enjoy it to the full. As an oily fish it spoils quickly. If it has been hauled out of the sea in a vast net, left to thrash around on deck, and then had a journey of several days to the supermarket, packed in ice, it will provide an ordinary meal. Line-caught and grilled within a few hours, the taste is unrivalled.

We saw plenty more wildlife during the rest of our time on the island, but after those two days in the north the recce had served its purpose. I already knew I'd be coming back for a longer stay. I spent as much time as I could outside, getting to know the place as thoroughly as possible. One afternoon, though, we were forced inside by sheeting rain and wind. As I had done on Skye (as I do in every holiday cottage), I took the chance to read through the visitor book. And as is always apparent, it was obvious that the slower pace of life on Colonsay appealed to others too. The same words and phrases reappeared throughout. People from all parts of Britain, and further afield, were refreshed and relaxed by the end of their stay. Batteries were recharged. Contrasts were repeatedly drawn between normal, everyday life with its noise, pollution, stresses and strains, and the lifestyle here with peace, tranquillity, calm, and sightings of interesting plants and animals. Families wrote about activities with their children that provided a meaningful connection with the natural world and would have been part of a routine, normal upbringing far more widely only a few decades ago. Wild flowers were picked, dunes were run down, long walks in the fresh air were taken, shells were collected, wild fruits or wild fish were gathered and eaten. For many of us, it seems, these have become things that we do once a year on the family holiday.

Perhaps it's not the sort of thing you write in a visitor book, but no-one seemed to miss the TV or be troubled by the lack of wi-fi. In fact, whenever these two things were mentioned, it was to point out how refreshing it was to be without them. I was struck especially by comments from people who loved the feeling of being without them, but acknowledged that this was only possible because temptation had been removed. If wi-fi is ever installed here, there will be fewer walks on the beach, fewer wild flowers picked, and more time spent checking in with the rest of humanity. I was reminded of an old quote by the American psychologist Rollo May from his book *The Cry for Myth*: 'technology is the knack of so arranging the world that we do not experience it.'* Although, written in 1991, this was a comment on the way things were three decades ago, it could also be seen as a prophecy for how much worse the levels of detachment from the real world would become in the early twenty-first century.

I've taken what I hope is not too great a liberty in reproducing here just a few of the comments from that visitor book:

> . . . the magic remains – the peace, the silence, the stunning views, the wildlife, the ever-changing light. (John and Valerie)

> We have visited few places that rival this wild and wonderful island in its beauty. The remoteness brought our family closer together. (Jacqueline)

---

* May, R. (1991) *The Cry for Myth*. W. W. Norton, New York.

. . . days of walking, bird-spotting, shell-collecting . . . just how relaxing can a place be? Going home relaxed and recharged. (Emma, Graham and Harriet)

Arrived. Mind emptied. Sun shone. Then set. Sea sparkled. Wind blew. Now we are leaving. (Anon.)

Our cameras are filled with pictures of children under giant skies in sublime landscapes. Everyday, every hour, we have been amazed by the unending, spectacular, crazy beauty of the island. (Asta, Bo, Nick and Rebekah)

What a delight it is to bring our two 'children' back to Colonsay where they each took their first steps 20 and 18 years ago. They still run on the beach, they still do head-stands and cartwheels, and manic frog-leaps from the dunes, and they still feel, as I do, at home here. (Alison)

After a couple of glasses of wine, looking out at the view and thinking of my own 'children', just a year or two younger, I found the last comment strangely moving. The words, like the other comments, were describing such simple and easy pleasures and yet they carried an unexpected power. If an alien race were trying to make sense of this visitor book, they might think that the people writing in it had stumbled upon an easy, inexpensive way of making their otherwise difficult lives more enjoyable, richer and fulfilling. They might reasonably wonder why fami-lies would come here for two weeks and undertake these activities, only to head back to their normal lives, ready to charge up their mobiles at the expense of their own freshly recharged batteries.

When I reflect on my first five decades of life it feels that I've repeatedly fallen into traps that make my relationship with wild-life (and my life more broadly) somewhat less fulfilling than it could have been. I know where the traps are and what they look like. I know how to avoid them, and that life is better for doing so. But much like all the people who had left comments in the visitor book, I keep walking into them and suffering the consequences. Despite our move to Devon and occasional trips like this one, I spend most of my time indoors, regularly checking in on the wider world through a screen of one sort or another. I remain more detached from close, meaningful contact with nature than I would like. I aspire to do better.

INDEX